Hollywood's Master Showman

Hollywood's Master Showman

The Legendary Sid Grauman

Charles Beardsley

NEW YORK CORNWALL BOOKS LONDON

Cornwall Books
440 Forsgate Drive
Cranbury, New Jersey 08512

Cornwall Books
25 Sicilian Avenue
London, WC1A 2QH, England

Cornwall Books
2133 Royal Windsor Drive
Unit 1
Mississauga, Ontario,
L5J 1K5, Canada

Library of Congress Cataloging in Publication Data

Beardsley, Charles.
    Hollywood's master showman.

    Includes index.
    1. Grauman, Sid, 1879-1950. 2. Theatrical managers—
United States—Biography. 3. Impresarios—United States—
Biography. 4. Moving-picture theaters—United States.
I. Title.
PN2287.G677B4   792'.092'4 [B]   80-69966
ISBN 0-8453-4703-9   AACR2

Printed in the United States of America

This book is gratefully dedicated to
Bruce W. LaLanne, artist, theater expert,
and friend. Without his tireless dili-
gence, perception, and truly monumental
organization of research data this project
could not have been completed.

Contents

Author's Note

In reviewing the extensive data on Sid Grauman for this text and photo essay, it soon became apparent that Grauman's public and private existence were interchangeable and coexistent. These chapters therefore aim to view Grauman through his work, which, after all, is the essence and measure of any individual.

It should also be emphasized that this is a survey of available Grauman memorabilia, not a full-scale biography of character. Occasionally several different versions of a particular event in Sid's life are given, notably where the actual details cannot be determined.

If the reader will consider this work a study of the Grauman Prologue in its myriad and fascinating forms, a clear portrait of Sid Grauman the individual will emerge. He was unique, a brilliant theatrical entrepreneur who was perfectly in tune with his times. He remains today as important an element of Hollywood cinema history as any of his more famous movie-making peers who were so lavishly celebrated in his various motion picture theaters.

Foreword

A year before Sid Grauman's death by coronary occlusion in 1950, the Friars' Club held a testimonial dinner to honor the seventy-year-old master showman who was frequently called "Mister Hollywood" by his friends and business associates, and with very good reason.

At the speakers' table in a news photo of the event published by the *Citizen News* of March 24, 1949, were Mack Sennett, Darryl Zanuck, Rupert Hughes, Joseph Schenck, Sid Grauman, Al Jolson, Charles B. Skouras, and Samuel Goldwyn. These men represented a reasonable cross section of the Hollywood power structure, past and current; they were pioneers in the development of motion pictures through Hollywood's Golden Age.

The Friars' Club affair wasn't pompous, nor was it the often bawdy roast that is given to the club's regular honored guests. "It was, in short," said Lloyd L. Sloan of the *Citizen News,* "a gathering of Grauman's good friends, those on the dais and many more at the dinner tables. And beyond words of praise which the speakers heaped on the guest of honor was the definite feeling that this man meant a great deal to these men and to an entire era of which they were and are a part. Sid Grauman last night tied all the words together with his fine climactic speech of the evening. . . ."

Sid spoke of his first days in show business, of how he and his father turned a Market Street storefront into San Francisco's Unique Theater, at which the first musical act was Jesse Lasky and his sister, and the starring attraction was Joe E. Brown. Grauman told of hiring Al Jolson who came for four weeks and stayed for a year and a half, and of the 1906 earthquake and fire from whose devastation Grauman and his father rose phoenixlike to the call of business with their canvas-top theater.

Charles Skouras then took the podium to declare that Sid Grauman was the barometer of entertainment, with a nation of imitators. "The Skouras brothers," confessed Charles, "would see what Sid was up to, then copy it for the National Theaters chain to stir up business. . . . Sid was an original, but he's always had a strong sense of the commercial. . . ."

On October 27, 1949, the Hollywood Chamber of Commerce sponsored another testimonial to Sid Grauman, a banquet in the Blossom Room of the Hollywood Roosevelt Hotel. Before the banquet, Lowell E. Redelings reported in the *Citizen News* on the coming event and paid homage to the Grauman character: "Besides Sid Grauman, the showman, there is the other Grauman—the humanitarian—not so well-known to the public. . . . To countless recipients of his generosity, however, Sid Grauman is a legend . . . of kindness and thoughtfulness to his fellow man. . . ."

This appreciation of Grauman's work aims to give the reader some firsthand insights into how he worked. In his field, as a person and an artist, he was the best of his kind.

Acknowledgments

First of all, my thanks to Bruce W. LaLanne, whose contribution to the making of this book was unique and indispensible.

Others who gave me their consideration and assistance were Spurgeon Marsh, Sid Grauman's personal secretary at the Million Dollar in 1919; Harold Cantrell, a Grauman friend; Emma and "Lindy" Lindesmith (Emma danced in a 1932 Prologue); Harry Prier for his generous contribution of early Egyptian Theater programs; Albert C. White, C. B. De Mille's special effects director on *King of Kings*; Edwin Lester, once a Prologue director and participant in the earliest Prologues; Mrs. Virginia Stankevich, dancer/actress in *King of Kings* Prologue, along with her husband, Steve; Bruce Torrence, grandson of actor Ernest Torrence, for his ready assistance with photos from his Hollywood collection; Eddie Cress for his strong support and suggestions; Stewart Brady, for his interview; Terry Helgesen for his permission to use photos from his Hollywood collection; and Marian Ettlinger for her Egyptian Theater data.

For indispensable reference material, special thanks must be extended to the editors, past and present, of *Variety, Motion Picture News, The Los Angeles Herald, The New York Times, The Los Angeles Examiner, The Los Angeles Times, The Hollywood Citizen News,* and *The Los Angeles Mirror. Silent Star* by Colleen Moore (New York: Doubleday, 1968) and *John Ford* by Andrew Sinclair (New York: Dial Press, 1979) were also helpful. Special thanks are extended to *Console Magazine*.

My thanks also to all the other kind folk who wrote or called me to offer information on the Grauman theaters that would otherwise never have come to light. Their support and cooperation all helped immeasurably in bringing this book to publication.

Photo Credits

A History of Sid Grauman's Theaters

1

SIDNEY Patrick Grauman was born on Saint Patrick's Day, March 17, 1879, in Indianapolis, Indiana. He was one of six children born to David J. and Rosa Grauman. Sid's show business career really began when David Grauman took the seventeen-year-old Sid along with him to Yukon Territory during the Gold Rush, where the older Grauman intended to stage a benefit show for sick gold miners, open up a small theater, and possibly do some lucrative mining on the side.

When David Grauman was forced by family illness to return to the United States, he left young Sid at Dawson, in charge of his indifferent business interests. Sid made friends easily, at one time recruiting the young Jack London to sell tickets and hawk programs for the theater. Sid became close to London and other famed Klondike characters who later moved on to great success: Tex Rickard, the sports promoter; Robert W. Service, the poet; and Wilson Mizner of Hollywood Brown Derby fame, among others.

When he was nineteen, Sid returned to his family in San Francisco. Not long afterwards he and his father opened their own theater, the Unique. Even then there were hints of the elegance that would later make Sid Grauman world-famous—

deep-carpeted steps, an ornate facade, a uniformed Chinese usher to greet arriving patrons. Later the Graumans hosted such talents as Erich von Stroheim, actor Frank Bacon (star of *Lightnin'*), singer Al Jolson, comedian Joe. E. Brown, nightclub entertainer Sophie Tucker, and a dancer named Baby Dolliver, the future mother of Jackie Coogan. Showmen Marcus Loew and Alexander Pantages borrowed ideas from the Graumans to launch their own theatrical careers.

When the flourishing Unique was destroyed by fire in the devastating 1906 San Francisco earthquake, dauntless Sid rented a large circus tent from a stranded evangelist, set it up on hastily cleared land, and advertised over the entrance: NOTHING TO FALL ON YOU EXCEPT CANVAS. This clever publicity device brought the Graumans immediate business.

After spending several more years in San Francisco and its environs, the Graumans moved to southern California, unable any longer to resist the siren call of Hollywood's golden promise. The story of Sid's rise to fame in Los Angeles is inseparable from the film industry's growth from the 1910s through the 1930s. Early motion picture exploitation on the grand scale is epitomized by the monumental magnificence of Grauman's Chinese Theater on Hollywood Boulevard, which is still operating under a different name in the 1980s as America's most distinguished remaining picture palace.

The venerable Chinese Theater was Sid's personal concept, developed in association with producer Joseph Schenck and tycoon Charles Toberman. The apocryphal story goes that Toberman kept enlarging the theater's plans beyond all practicality, until Grauman and Schenck finally conspired to ship him off to the Orient to gather authentic data. Meanwhile, the two partners went ahead with groundbreaking on April 10, 1926. The beautiful silent screen star Norma Talmadge turned the first spadeful of earth at the Chinese site with a gold-plated shovel before a crowd of officials, fans, and the entire cast from the Prologue of King Vidor's *The Big Parade*, which was then playing down the boulevard at Sid Grauman's Hollywood Egyptian Theater. Charles Toberman took such a long time researching Chinese art and architecture that he missed the formal opening of the Chinese Theater, which was held on May 19, 1927, exactly one year, one month, and nine days after his departure for the Orient.

Grauman chose for his opening feature the long-awaited and highly publicized Cecil B. De Mille production of the Christ story, *King of Kings*, which starred H. B. Warner. It was the first time that the face of Jesus had ever been portrayed in a film. Controversy raged over the tastefulness of the film until the reviews came in, all unanimous raves. Praise was as loud for Grauman's stupendous Prologue that introduced the film as for De Mille's masterpiece. Keen at arranging spectacles, Grauman outdid himself this time.

On the night of May 18, one day before public showings of *King of Kings* began, a special invitational premiere was staged before a select Hollywood audience of 2,000 people. It is safe to say that in the history of cinema there has never been such an illustrious gathering of luminaries for a Hollywood gala. All of the movie industry's most important people were there.

An estimated crowd of from 24,000 to 50,000 (not the biggest spectator count Grauman ever commanded; that would come later) jammed Hollywood Boulevard for blocks around the Chinese Theater to catch glimpses of their favorite stars arriving by limousine. Ribs were broken in the

Left to right: **Henry Duffy of the Henry Duffy Players, financier C. E. Toberman, and Sid Grauman, at the El Capitan Theater in Hollywood (1927).**

crush, women fainted, and youths fought savagely for the best vantage points along the crowded route. The premiere was a glittering, three-ring circus brilliantly produced by Sid Grauman, and, as one historian wryly observes, with equal billing given to Grauman, De Mille, and Christ, in that pecking order.

The Prologue was scheduled to get underway at 8:30 p.m., with the film to follow. Both productions were to be preceded by a special one-time presentation, which was also Grauman's brainchild. Highlights of this presentation included the appearance of Fred Niblo, director of *Ben Hur*, who, in turn, presented filmdom's cinema master, David Wark Griffith. Griffith then introduced Will Hays, the motion picture censor czar, who presented the ultimate attraction, Mary Pickford, America's Sweetheart, whose sobriquet, incidentally, was David Grauman's much earlier inspiration. Miss Pickford pressed a jade button, the great curtains parted, and the Prologue began.

Prologues were already a unique, well-established specialty of Sid Grauman's show-biz genius ever since he inaugurated them at his downtown Los Angeles Million Dollar Theater in 1918. Grau-

A grouping for one of the dramatic tableaux in the 1927 prologue for *King of Kings* at Grauman's Chinese Theater.

Conductor Bakaleinikoff with two members of the *Kings of Kings* prologue cast during 1927 dress rehearsals at Grauman's Chinese Theater.

Actors from the prologue *King of Kings* rehearsing atop the newly completed Grauman's Chinese Theater (1927).

man had created the movie Prologue for American audiences, along with the red carpet and searchlight premiere. His considerable talent lay in matching the thematic material of the Prologue to the movie that was to follow. By offering a vivid, live cornucopia of sight, sound, and colorful movement to introduce the principal elements of the upcoming film, Grauman prepared the audience for the film's atmosphere and its stars.

The Prologue for *King of Kings* was spectacular, solemnly biblical, and certainly no gaudy vaudeville circuit extravaganza, as the Prologues frequently were. This Prologue contained enough reverence to satisfy even the most rabid religious purist. The evangelical Aimee Semple McPherson, herself a theatrical wizard, praised it volubly from her pulpit.

The cast of the Prologue of over one hundred players was handpicked by Grauman. The master scene entitled "The Meeting Place of the Populace" was composed of several segments: "Twilight Prayers of the Common People," and "Dance of the Ebony Slave," featuring a solo by Maurice Mor-

gan. The next scene was "The Chant of the Israelite Priests," which was followed by "The Holy City," poignantly sung by Stewart Brady, a stocky, lyrical boy soprano dressed as a shepherd, who was backed by a full symphony orchestra.

The wide range of richly detailed biblical costumes used in the Prologue was designed by MGM costumer Adrian, and the pit orchestra played appropriate music composed for the occasion by the Bakaleinikoff brothers. Skillfully directed, the Prologue scenes were designed to blend seamlessly into the motion picture credits of one of the most successful films in all motion picture history, a film that is still shown in Christian churches round the world during religious holidays.

Spectacularly staged and enthusiastically received by the star-studded preview audience, the Prologue lasted so long that the feature was not screened until 11:00 P.M., and then continued for nearly three hours. It is claimed that De Mille became so irritated at the length of the program that he vowed never to open another film in Hollywood.

Main set for the prologue to *King of Kings*, **Grauman's Chinese Theater (1927).**

Detail from master shot of the Last Supper scene in Cecil B. De Mille's production of *King of Kings*, starring H. B. Warner.

Grauman worked continuously in all of his many Prologue presentations to carry the audience further than any of his imitators ever could. He would go to almost any extreme to get just the right acts and players to reinforce the theme of the accompanying film. His extravagance was well known from coast to coast, and the Prologues were often better than the films.

The Prologues were greatly enhanced by the settings in which they were staged, for the several Grauman movie palaces were astonishing visual creations. Audiences flocked to a Grauman show at a Grauman theater because they knew they would enter into fantasy land through the front portals and could watch an exciting Prologue and a first-rate film in plush opera chairs amid tasteful surroundings.

The luxurious Chinese Theater was the ultimate movie house, as that first bedazzled audience vouched. It was apparent by word-of-mouth and next day's press on May 20, 1927, that Sid Grauman had outdone even his own previous lush spectacles. The carefully chosen guests at the premiere who crowded into the massive movie house were as impressed by what they saw inside as were the fans who gathered before the theater's exotic exterior facade.

Outside, the green bronze pagoda roof towered some ninety feet above the splendid forecourt with its entrance portico of jade bronze, flanked on either side by two cinnabar-red pillars. Beneath these pillars stood two large stone dogs ferociously guarding the entrance to the temple. A bronze statue in front of the stone dogs symbolized the human genius of poetry and drama. The statue was surrounded by flames that signified eternal creative imagination, another of Grauman's inspirations.

(The idea of the world-famous signatures and footprints of movie stars, which have helped keep the Chinese Theater a landmark through its fifty-two years of existence and into current ownership by Mann's Theaters, was yet to be developed.) Gone now are the tall Chinese sentries who patrolled the forecourt's parapet before each performance, a gimmick that Grauman had previously employed on the Egyptian's roof for several years in the form of Arab sentries in flowing costumes pacing with long rifles.

The spacious interior of the Chinese Theater was even more dazzling than its exterior. A central sunburst pendant chandelier hung sixty feet above the rows of plush lounge seats. The auditorium was flame red with accents of jade and gold. Side walls that could be glimpsed behind tawny columns were paneled with classic antique Chinese art reproductions. All seats, as in the Egyptian, were located on a single raked floor, and every seat offered a clear view of the stage and screen. Beside the rear projection booth wall were luxurious celebrity boxes for special visitors where they could see but not be seen.

The massive fireproof proscenium curtain was designed to represent the twin doors of a huge Chinese cabinet, decorated with figures on a peacock blue field. Even the great curtain's rise was properly dramatic, the pace so leisurely that its upward movement was almost hypnotic.

Today, the cumulative effect of the recently revitalized auditorium upon the uninitiated tourist can be as breathtaking as it was that opening night. Missing, however, is the large corps of ushers and usherettes costumed in richly worked Chinese robes of classic design. Standing beneath minispotlights at various stations throughout the house to guide patrons to their reserved seats, they added an authentic note of quiet dignity to the atmosphere of the house that Grauman had so painstakingly created.

Sid Grauman's most enduring publicity brainchild was born with the Chinese Theater. According to one legend, Norma Talmadge happened to step into a block of wet concrete while visiting the theater site during its construction, leaving her footprint thereon. This incident is supposed to have given Grauman the idea for the forecourt's famed celebrity prints.

In another story, possibly apocryphal but still circulating, Grauman's good friend Douglas Fairbanks, Sr., bought a Los Angeles property in 1927 called Rancho Zorro after one of his most famous roles and was remodeling it into a fantasy hacienda. One of the first improvements that Doug ordered for the property was an irrigation dam. As Doug and his wife Mary Pickford were inspecting the construction of the dam, they sat down beside some freshly laid concrete, pressed their hands into it and wrote their names. From this touching moment, says their biographer Gary Carey, came the inspiration for Sid's sumptuous new Chinese Theater forecourt. Why not place the handprints and footprints of stars outside the building, thus creating publicity for the stars and a magnet to draw the public?

Considering Grauman's quick and fecund mind, the actual origin of the prints in the Chinese Theater's forecourt is probably the following. During the construction of the theater, its contractor Rudolf Liebold employed a skilled mason named Jean Klossner who was descended from a long line of European stonemasons dating back to medieval times and the building of Notre Dame in Paris. Klossner traditionally left his handprint as his signature at every job he completed. Grauman's keen eye caught Klossner's handprint on an inspection tour and he questioned Klossner about it. The showman soon learned that a special concrete recipe was needed to retain prints of any sort, and Klossner's personal mix was his carefully guarded professional secret.

Grauman was immediately intrigued. Why not immortalize the stars who had appeared at his theater in film and flesh in the forecourt concrete slabs, to preserve them for posterity? Grauman made arrangements with Klossner to mix concrete slabs on order. The mason needed three days to prepare his chemical formula properly. He kept the formula in a safe and frequently haggled with Grauman at the last minute over his fee.

In 1928, when Grauman refused to meet Klossner's price and hired another concrete artist to enshrine Jean Hersholt (the actor of "Dr. Christian" fame) and his perennial pipe in the forecourt, the actor's prints crumbled away in less than a month. Not until 1949, a year before Grauman's death, was Hersholt enshrined permanently in the Chinese forecourt.

An impressive list of filmdom greats have been processed into the Chinese forecourt's concrete slabs. Italian superstar Sophia Loren was once flown in from Rome just for the ceremony. A World War II paratrooper named Joe Bran was chosen to leave his footprints along with those of aquatic pinup girl Esther Williams. The event, declared Bran, was a lot more exciting than any parachute jump he had made over enemy territory.

Not only footprints and handprints were set in the forecourt concrete. Gene Autry brought his horse, Champion, which required that a special clean-up crew be in close attendance while the hoofprints were taken. Al Jolson's knee is there in his famous "Mammy" song pose. The great John Barrymore's profile lies on horizontal display. Edgar Bergen brought Charlie McCarthy so that the dummy's monocle could be imprinted. Tom Mix's ten-gallon hat is there in silhouette. Harold Lloyd's glasses, Harpo Marx's harp, Betty Grable's famous legs, even Sonja Henie's ice skates are all on permanent exhibit for the 1.5 million tourists, many of them European and Japanese, who flock to the Chinese forecourt each year.

A rumor persists that someone stole the prints of Charlie Chaplin, which were placed in the forecourt in 1928. Although the management denies this, Chaplin is no longer represented among the immortals.

After Julie Andrews's legs got stuck briefly in the wet concrete, a one-foot-at-a-time policy was laid down. The Chinese Theater carries accident insurance to cover anyone who might stub a toe on the famous impressions, as one patron did over Greer Garson's size-7 footprint. A ritual that started as one of Grauman's throwaway novelties has since become a celebrated, world-renowned tourist magnet.

The Grauman name, however, no longer greets Chinese Theater patrons and tourists as they approach the august cinema shrine. Currently the theater is owned and operated by movie producer and exhibitor Ted Mann, the exclusive stockholder of the 300-house motion picture chain that carries his name nationally. Despite the marquee change, film buffs young and old all know whose original vision made the theater unique in 1927, and many of them still call it Grauman's Chinese. Most of these aficionados are also familiar with the fact that Sid Grauman lent his distinguished show-biz name and acumen to the creation of several other film houses in the Los Angeles area: The Million Dollar and the Rialto theaters, both on downtown Broadway; the Metropolitan Theater, later the Paramount, now a

site for the Jewelry Center, at Sixth and Hill streets; and the Hollywood Egyptian on Hollywood Boulevard a few blocks east of the Chinese.

Ted Mann, who is married to film star Rhonda Fleming, has kept the faith with myriad Grauman fans by restoring the Chinese Theater to its original splendor. Mann has recently acquired the property just east of, and adjacent to, the Chinese Theater on which he has built two new movie houses, Chinese II and Chinese III, which opened in 1979. Mann has continued the Grauman tradition of luxury by installing the finest sound equipment available and three-inch padded opera chairs in both 750-person houses.

"By chopping the Chinese up into three small units I could have saved half of the $3 million it cost me to build Chinese II and Chinese III," Mann has said. "But the Chinese Theater is second only to Disneyland as a prime tourist attraction in southern California and I was morally obliged to preserve it as a historical landmark."

The two new houses of Oriental design opened April 12, 1979, with a highly publicized, red carpet premiere of Dino de Laurentiis's *Hurricane*, a remake of the 1930s Dorothy Lamour and Jon Hall South Sea epic. The gala, a fifty-dollar per ticket benefit for the Hollywood Historic Trust, with a Polynesian supper party afterwards, was attended by many celebrities.

Sid Grauman's collective presentations at his various southern California movie houses were a vital factor in the spread of the popularity of motion pictures not only on the West Coast but also nationally and internationally. The Grauman name is synonymous with sterling entertainment. Grauman paid such attention to the setting of even the most trivial vehicle that no theatergoer ever felt that he or she hadn't gotten his or her money's worth. There will probably never be another Hollywood impresario with the quality of show-biz magic that Grauman brought to whatever he touched. One needn't be a nostalgia freak to acknowledge filmdom's and the public's debt to this legendary innovator. The Grauman era was precisely right for Sid's special brand of savoir faire. As one writer has observed, Grauman was to silent movie palaces what P. T. Barnum was to circuses. Only Flo Ziegfeld of "Follies" fame managed to upstage Sid Grauman in theater extravaganzas, but even Ziegfeld never attempted the motion picture Prologue.

Starting as an adolescent in show business,

Grauman finished his theatrical career shortly before his death in 1950 at the age of seventy. He had an active hand in the managing of the Chinese Theater right up to his final illness. To appreciate the inimitable star quality of Grauman's work, it is necessary to know something of the man and to savor his intense dedication to the arts, his many kindnesses, his enduring loyalty to friends, and his exceptional ability to act upon an inexhaustible imagination and turn his dream fantasies into stunning theatrical realities. In today's national theater field, for comparison, there is only one entrepreneur who possesses the singular kind of vision that Sid Grauman so consistently exhibited. This man is producer and director Hal Prince, whose Broadway productions of the Stephen Sondheim musicals and other works are as superbly original as were Grauman's.

Known far and wide during his lifetime as "Little Sunshine," Sid Grauman was a soft-spoken, dedicated mover, a man who was always too busy developing his endless concepts to make serious enemies, and whose friends were legion. Toward the end of his life, Louella O. Parsons wrote of him: "Sid doesn't drink or smoke. He is very generous with his friends and spends large sums of money on expensive gifts for them. He has kept his friends all his life. Sid turns night into day and seldom goes to bed until dawn, then sleeps until late afternoon. While he played himself in a recent motion picture he stayed up all night so he wouldn't be late for the call. . . . If anyone gets a good spot 'Up There' it will be Sidney Grauman, master showman. . . ."

Grauman was close to many of Hollywood's first great stars: Douglas Fairbanks, Mary Pickford, Charlie Chaplin, Gloria Swanson, John Gilbert, George O'Brien, and a long line of great directors and producing moguls including D. W. Griffith, King Vidor, John Ford, James Cruze, Jesse Lasky, Joseph Schenck, Louis B. Mayer, and Irving Thalberg, among others. One of the reasons for Grauman's enduring success was the friendly cooperation that stars and executives were willing to give him because of his constant readiness to offer them a favor without a thought of its return.

Sid Grauman was a stickler for authenticity in the decor of his various theaters and in his many Prologues. Although he admired movies with near reverence, he had the innate good sense to remain with what he did best and shied away from film production. Grauman was in only two films, enacting cameo roles in Deanna Durbin's movie *Mad about Music*, in which he played himself, and with Clark Gable in *Call of the Wild*, in which he played a casino dealer in the Yukon, a part for which he needed no briefing.

Sid Grauman's personal success story is also an integral part of the birth and growth of American cinema and must be filtered through its historical context to appreciate his accomplishment. He was an American original who roundly deserves to be remembered for his multiple talents, his ability to realize his ideas, his warm personality, and the glamour that he brought to the motion picture industry during Hollywood's golden era.

2

"SHOWMANSHIP is like any other merchandising," Sid Grauman told an interviewer on January 4, 1931, in Los Angeles, four years after the brilliant opening of the Chinese Theater. "You must first buy desirable material, then present it to attractive advantage, and price it right. . . . Above all, you must let the whole world know what you have to sell. . . ."

Eight years earlier, at the time the Egyptian Theater opened, a Los Angeles publicist wrote a piece on Sid Grauman in which the impresario stated that any man who could accurately gauge the public's taste—and thereby select with infallible wisdom exactly what theatergoers wanted—might become a multimillionaire easily within a couple of years.

Sid Grauman called such a phenomenon an impossible press-agent's dream.

"The public," Sid declared, "doesn't *demand* anything. It makes no request of producers and it doesn't whisper its tastes to the most alert of exhibitors—not until *after* the event.

"For example, the public didn't demand *The Miracle Man* or *Find That Woman*"—two of Grauman's greatest successes at the Million Dollar:

It waited until some producer had the wit and good taste to create these pictures. And only after looking at them did it decide that it wanted them.

Other pictures in close imitation of the two films aforementioned may be made with the idea that, by following the public's expressed desires, they will also enjoy a wide popularity. But of course they may fail, for by the time they're released the fickle public may have taken a notion to attend some other type of entertainment.

To make what I mean very plain [Sid continued], I cite electricity. The public didn't demand electrical power at first—it didn't even know that any such force existed. It remained for genius to discover, harness and deliver the power—*then* the public bought telephones, telegrams, transportation and industrial power. The same is true of automobiles. Only a few experts saw the enormous potential of gasoline engines, put them into buggies, and the public quickly forgot that there ever was a creature called a horse.

It is only after a thing is created that the public demands it. If it were possible to consult the public and discover what it wants, the showman's job would be easy. But until that time he must work in the dark, explore uncharted seas, take large chances. The wisest thing an exhibitor can do is to align himself with producers who make pictures that the public often surprises itself by demanding.

Modest as always, Grauman was giving the production companies more credit perhaps than they deserved. Actually his own instinct for public taste was almost unerringly on target. What he probably meant to imply during the interview was that he followed the film production market with astute sharp-eyed attention. He chose the films that he exhibited from the movie companies whose films most nearly paralleled the public's taste, and then presented these films in the most beguiling and tasteful atmosphere that his considerable showmanship could create. If Grauman did not always find the hit movie that the public was ready to embrace, his brilliant Prologue presentations compensated to such an extent that sometimes it was the framing of the pictures at his various theaters that the public came primarily to see.

Grauman's initial foray into show business, according to legend, occurred when he was a mere adolescent. If his mother, Rosa, had not been the pragmatic, inventive woman that she was, Sid Grauman might never have attended his first party at the age of fourteen or become aware that he had a talent for theatrical invention.

The incident took place in a small, anonymous Colorado mining town in the 1890s where D. J. Grauman was involved in mining interests. At that time young Sid had never been to a party. His father disliked social gatherings, his mother didn't have time for them, with six children to raise. But when a certain young lady from a wealthy family announced that she was having a birthday party and he was invited, young Sid decided that he must attend at all costs. The day before the party, however, Sid realized that the event was to be a dress-up affair, and alas, he had no presentable clothes. In fact, he was still in short pants and knickers, and these were not very new.

In a dejected mood, Sid told his mother about his predicament. Rosa could not buy the boy a new suit; they had very little money in those days, and besides, no ready-made clothes were available on short notice in the small town where they lived. Undaunted, Rosa rummaged through an old trunk and found a much-worn suit cast off by David. She ripped it up, washed and ironed the pieces, and cut and sewed them into a presentable garment for Sid. His mother stayed up all night before the party in order to make Sid a stylish suit.

On the eve of the party, Sid donned his new clothes, studied himself in the mirror, and was de-

lighted with the results. "I looked as good as any kid in town, if you didn't inspect for details," Sid was fond of pointing out whenever he told the story. He kissed Rosa gratefully and told her she was his fairy godmother and he would make her proud of him yet.

That night Sid went to the party. A touring pianist provided some solid classical music, which Sid enjoyed—his mother was an accomplished pianist but rarely had the time to play. As the party progressed Sid remained unobtrusively in the background. But later in the evening, when things began to slowly lose their party momentum and boredom seemed imminent, Sid found himself moving through the crowd, asking if anyone did recitations or played a musical instrument. It was not long before Sid put a young lady on the town hall platform to recite humorous poems while he found a rustic violinist and a harmonica player who were glad to improvise rudimentary dance music. Sid saw to it that people had enough punch and that everyone knew everyone else, and eventually when the dancing palled, he led the partygoers in communal games. When the affair finally broke up, Sid was congratulated by the young hostess for his ingenuity, and slapped on the back by his male friends. He had found his element as unofficial host of what turned out to be the jolliest event of the year, giving the townspeople small talk for days afterwards.

Sid came home from the party flushed with success and a new sense of leadership. He realized that he had a very real ability to cater to people's tastes, to know instinctively what they wanted. This may well have been his first conscious awareness that he could please the public. Up to that time he had lived a roving life with his parents and siblings. D. J. Grauman had tried many jobs, among them touring a troupe called Georgia's Minstrels through the Midwest. At another time he was a railroad man, which kept him on the move, so that young Sid attended schools in Boston, Chicago, and various other cities around the country. The Graumans also lived in Washington, D.C., for a while.

In the nation's capital when Sid was nine years old he saw his first grand shows. He sold librettos at the opera house and was caught up at once in the magic of the productions, almost forgetting to work as he watched that wonderful, bewildering spectacle of music and drama for the first time.

"After that," Sid later explained, "whenever I

was missing from my home, my mother could always find me around some stage door. I was hooked for life, so it was natural enough for me to step forward the night of that Colorado party and help get things going."

From Colorado, as one source claims, the whole family moved to Alaska in the late 1890s, at the time of the Yukon Gold Rush. Other sources place Rosa and the children in Seattle or San Francisco, probably the latter, while David and young Sid made the trek North, sans family.

Father and son went through all sorts of hardships and dangers in Alaska. There was the grueling winter march over formidable Chilkoot Pass, and shooting the White Horse Rapids in a leaky scow. While traveling to Dawson with his father was an exciting adventure for Sid, the rigorous, grubby existence of Yukon life under Gold Rush conditions was not precisely the get-rich-quick dream come true that had originally lured the pair to Yukon Territory with high hopes of making their fortune.

Illness, a scarcity of fresh supplies and their outrageous costs, plus the foul weather—malarial, humid summers and winter blizzards—all contributed to the Graumans' ebbing faith that they would make their fortune. But the Yukon did spark Sid's creativity; he had the knack of making impossible situations work for him. The Graumans somehow managed to produce an occasional variety show under the crudest of conditions. Sid sold West Coast newspapers, long-outdated, at fancy prices to the miners. Even the local Dawson paper, called *The Nugget* by the newsboys, was about the size of a theatrical program and sold for twenty-five cents.

Sid's truly first professional theatrical enterprise was the holding of a benefit for Dawson's newsboys. They were having a tough winter because the statewide papers were not getting through because of an exceptionally heavy snowfall.

Sid secured some very good talent for the benefit, for he had discovered on checking around carefully that there were quite a few erstwhile theatrical folk seeking their fortunes in Alaskan gold. He found some talented bar girls working the dance halls who were only too glad to get up on a makeshift stage and exhibit their charms. Without proper costumes for a real show, Sid recruited clothes wherever he could find them, often knocking on

doors to beg the loan of an opera hat, a pair of long kid gloves, a fan, or a brocaded shawl. Sid's Dawson follies benefit was a huge success and netted about $1,200 for the newsboys.

Unfortunately, there are all too few verifiable details about the Dawson period in Sid's life. In later years he recounted many amusing yarns of those Yukon days and nights. Most of these were harmless embellishments on the truth, for Sid was a natural-born storyteller. One source has suggested that some of the finest sight gags in Charlie Chaplin's *The Gold Rush* were inspired by Grauman's fund of Yukon tales.

It is a fact, however, that David Grauman received somber news from home. One of Sid's sisters had fallen seriously ill in San Francisco and his father departed, leaving Sid alone in Dawson with very little cash and no parental guidance. The decision to leave Sid in Alaska must have been a harrowing one for the elder Grauman to make. The two had always been close, more like brothers than father and son. But apparently there was only enough money for one of the Graumans to make the trip, and D. J. must have felt that it was his responsibility to go home. This decision was probably not without encouragement from Sid, for even as a teenager Sid was bright and mature enough to handle independent existence with his usual sparkling enthusiasm, up to a point, of course.

D. J. Grauman was never to return to Dawson. Sid continued to live there on his own, but he was not without friends and protectors, as we shall see. Even guardians, however, could not fully protect Sid from his lifelong Achilles' heel, which was gambling. At one point in Sid's solo Dawson days he lost his entire stake to a Yukon card shark.

Actress June Lockhart tells this story about Sid's passion for gambling: "When I was a little girl of eleven, I used to spend a great deal of time with my best girl friend, Jackie Paley, daughter of Jay Paley, in Holmby Hills. . . . I remember on more than one occasion when Jackie and I would come down for breakfast, the 'grown-up' poker game begun the night before was still going on—once, we were told, because Mr. Grauman had gambled away the Chinese Theater and the guests were playing until he won it back. Constance Bennett was often one of the card players. . . ."

Cold, miserably ill with malaria, and often hungry as well as homesick, Sid was about to give up when a kindly grubstaker, who had to leave town in a hurry because he had just passed some bad checks, generously gave Sid his shipment of the first newspapers arriving on the next freighter from the States. The shipment contained 2,000 newspapers and Sid was ecstatic at this unexpected windfall. He planned to sell the papers in Dawson at a dollar each to the miners and then get out of Alaska as quickly as he could before his profits were gone.

Hearing of Sid's unexpected good luck, the young Wilson Mizner approached Sid with an ingenious plan. He would give Sid twenty-five dollars (one source says fifty dollars) for a single newspaper copy, providing that Sid would hold off selling his papers for an hour. Mizner had rented a storeroom and intended to charge two hundred miners one dollar apiece to sit and listen to him give a dramatic reading of news from home. Sid liked the idea and agreed to the bargain. After Mizner's reading of the news highlights, Sid sold all of his papers in short order.

Instead of leaving Dawson, Sid took his $2,000 nest egg and went into business for himself, his gambler's instinct ever active. There is no precise record of how Sid parlayed his $2,000 into $6,000, the amount he was supposed to have carried with him out of the Yukon, but presumably he marketed whatever commodities he could find to sell, at a cash advantage. Two years after his arrival in the Yukon with his father, the nineteen-year-old Sid Grauman sailed for San Francisco.

At this point the sources differ. One claims that Sid lost most of his stake aboard ship to professional gamblers, and arrived in San Francisco almost penniless. This tale is probably close to the truth, for Sid went to work the moment he landed in San Francisco as a ticket taker, errand boy, and janitor at the Cinemagraph Theater where he viewed his first motion picture. He was deeply impressed with the novelty, but even more enthusiastic about its commercial potential, for films were already a powerful magnet to the curious public.

In San Francisco Sid was reunited with D. J., Rosa, and the Grauman children. He continued to work at the Cinemagraph for a while, and it was during this period that Sid determined to make show business his life's career. He had already learned the hard way in Alaska that ingenuity in packaging a product for public purchase made all the difference between success and failure.

Sid began to study ways and means to enhance the presentation of the new "flickers" at the Cinemagraph. When he told his father about the impressive box-office returns that piled up daily, both father and son gave serious thought to films. Dapper D. J. Grauman began to share his son's enthusiasm for the medium, and the two finally decided that the only sure way to success in the business was to own and operate their own theater.

D. J. and Sid found an appropriate location for their theater in a building called the Hoodoo Store because everybody who set up in business there had bad luck. Financing the theater was the critical problem; the Graumans had very little cash. The legend goes that David Grauman ran a classified ad in a San Francisco daily, in which he asked for the loan of $5,000—a considerable sum in those days—with which to back an enterprise described as "catering to men, ladies and children." D. J. Grauman received only a single reply but it paid off handsomely. A caller agreed to back the Graumans for half of the theater's profits, an acceptable arrangement. The Unique Theater was thus born.

D. J. and Sid Grauman built a slanting floor to afford their patrons an unimpeded view of the stage. There was no fly gallery, so scenery rolled up and down. Next to the theater lobby the Graumans constructed the first freestanding box office. They opened by showing films from France and were an immediate hit. Any old film was a marvel in those days, especially an "imported" one, so the house was always filled with patrons. Sid soon began to exhibit American films. To him belongs the honor of the premiere showing in the West of the movies' first feature film, The Great Train Robbery, which caused a sensation.

Weeks passed after the opening of the Unique Theater, and the Graumans' silent partner did not put in an appearance to collect his share of the profits. Since the Graumans had no information on him—they had merely collected the $5,000 at a specified bank—they were forced to wait for their patron to make himself known.

Finally, months later, as Sid stood in front of the theater one night, he noticed a furtive figure slip out of the shadows across the street and stand on the curb to peer over at the Unique's billboards. Sid's instinct told him it was their phantom backer. Sid yelled at him, but the man hurried off. Sid sent the doorman after him, and the doorman returned with the reluctant partner's card. The following day D. J. Grauman called on their silent partner.

The backer himself answered the door and told D. J. that he was a very wealthy man whose invalid wife was given to quixotic philanthropy. The couple had seen the Graumans' ad and the wife had begged her husband to investigate. The couple liked the novel idea of the Unique Theater, but for personal reasons they did not wish to share in the profits. D. J. Grauman persuaded his benefactors to accept at least the return of their investment, although they stoutly refused to take anything else. According to Sid in later years, this marked the beginning of the Grauman fortune, once estimated at $14 million. It goes without saying that Sid was never again in a monetary bind.

If one interprets this version of the Graumans' debut in film business as just another of Sid's tall tales, then one must accept as fact that Sid actually did return to San Francisco with his $6,000 nest egg from the Yukon still intact, and that it was this amount that established the Graumans in their first San Francisco business venture. Whatever the truth, the Graumans did open the Unique Theater with resounding success from the very start, mainly because it was different and offered what the public obviously wanted to see. To create cheap entertainment that pleased the already sophisticated San Francisco palate was no mean feat in a city that attracted the world's prime opera, ballet, drama, and variety stars from the international scene to its stages: the great Enrico Caruso, Edwin Booth, Sarah Bernhardt, opera singer Dame Nellie Melba, Lotta Crabtree, Oscar Wilde, and Lola Montez, to name but a few.

In the years before the 1906 earthquake and fire, the Graumans exhibited films and simple acts at the Unique. There were seven shows a day on weekdays (some say fifteen), and the admission charge was ten cents a customer. The performances lasted approximately twenty-five minutes. Many entertainers who later became world-famous were associated with the Unique in its early days, and later with the Lyceum, the second Grauman house. Sid had, even in those days, the uncanny ability to pick exceptional talent.

It can be assumed that D. J. Grauman was probably content to continue operating the two theaters at a comfortable profit without further expansion. He certainly did not share Sid's dauntless enthusiasm and determination to expand the the-

atrical horizon of their lives with new challenges. Sid cast a speculative eye on San Jose, Stockton, and Sacramento as investment possibilities. He traveled in these areas and explored possible sites as well as audience potential.

The Unique and the Lyceum were very successful houses, but the Graumans were virtually wiped out by the 1906 disaster. Sid, however, resourceful as always, found the ideal solution to what might have remained a tragedy.

"The quake and fire hit us hard," Sid said in a 1923 interview many years later, "as it did thousands of other businessmen and residents. Both of our theaters burned down and we had no insurance in those days. After the fire we found a tent that some itinerant cowboy evangelist was willing to sell for $2,000, and pews to seat about 3,000 persons. We built a stage on the Unique's site, hooked up a tent to it, advertised its obvious safety features and called the new house Grauman's National Theater. It was just around the corner from Market Street, so we hired a barker to stand on Market and announce our programs." The Grauman policy was to present six acts of vaudeville with short films. The Graumans held continuous performances in the tent theater, while their well-known slogan, Nothing to Fall on You except Canvas, guaranteed the patrons' safety in case of another trembler.

"We showed live acts and pictures," Grauman elaborated, "and entertained 10,000 patrons a day. Admission was twenty-five cents. Patrons sat on the preacher's pews, the floor was earth covered with sawdust. The National ran for two years. Then we built a new theater over the canvas top and never lost a single performance. That theater stood until 1922."

Before long the Grauman name was an important one in San Francisco entertainment. Artists were anxious to work for Sid and his father. One of the first job applicants was an eager young singer with a dynamic personality and a good voice, which, however, lacked the power to project to the rear of the tent. The Graumans built a special thrust platform for the young singer who obligingly knelt down before the front rows of patrons to deliver his sentimental ballads. Al Jolson was an instant success and earned sixty dollars a week.

Another youngster who got his start with the Graumans was Joe E. Brown, the wide-mouthed comedian with the machine-gun delivery who displayed his eccentric brand of clowning to frequent-

Grauman's Tent Theater in San Francisco (1907).

ly startled yet always delighted audiences. The young Sophie Tucker perfected the singing act that would make her one of entertainment's brightest stars over the next fifty years.

It was no accident that many performers who became top show business personalities were showcased early in a Grauman theater. Sid's natural instinct could spot talent in a crowd of seemingly ordinary performers. It has been said that Sid had a Geiger counter for a nose and could detect the uranium of star quality in an instant.

As the Graumans grew more successful, expansion was inevitable to Stockton, Sacramento, and San Jose. The Graumans built the Empress Theater on Market Street, and later built the Strand Theater, which subsequently became the St. Francis Theater.

Sid was constantly on the lookout for new ways to publicize the San Jose theater, the Bijou. One night at a German beer garden in San Jose Sid heard a rotund singing waiter do his turn. He liked the singer's great style and outstanding grace, and the nonchalance with which he would balance six beer mugs in one hand while performing. Sid hired Roscoe "Fatty" Arbuckle to sing at the Bijou for $35 a week. Arbuckle insisted on one free dinner each day in addition to his weekly salary; this had been part of his working arrangement with the beer garden. Since Arbuckle had a prodigious appetite, it was easy to see why he made this demand.

Sid agreed reluctantly to the stipulation because he did not want to lose Arbuckle, whose comic talent—as well as his gifted singing—was readily apparent to Grauman. Sid did some fast thinking and made a deal with a Greek restaurant to provide Fatty with his daily dinner on the condition that Arbuckle had to eat this meal behind the restaurant's large plate-glass window in full view of the street. The spectacle was bizarre. Pedestrians were soon jamming the sidewalk outside the restaurant nightly to watch the brilliant pantomimist ingest the equivalent of five normal-sized dinners at one sitting, with inspired comic invention.

The restaurant picked up Arbuckle's tab and gained many new customers. Sid got himself some excellent free publicity for the Bijou, while Arbuckle was on his way to a bright future. He later became one of the most popular comedians ever to grace the silent screen, but his career came to a swift and tragic ending when he was tried for the alleged rape-murder of party girl Virginia Rappe in a sensational, grossly mispublicized San Francisco courtroom melodrama.

Sid spent eight years working out of the Graumans' San Francisco headquarters in partnership with his father. He began to look further afield than California for business challenges, and at length set his sights on New York.

After selling the Bijou Theater for $30,000, Sid took the train for New York. He opened a theater on 125th Street, the first four-a-day house that New York City had known, and modeled it along the same lines as the Unique. Although Sid fared well enough in New York and made some staunch lifelong friends, he decided eventually that the East was not for him. He sold his New York theater and returned to San Francisco where he felt more at home than anywhere else. Years later Sid told a Los Angeles interviewer about his New York debut.

"We had a tough time opening," Sid declared in 1923, "due to great rivalry from the other Manhattan houses. But our big day finally came, and after a good dress rehearsal all the acts left to rest. When the theater opened that night not a single act showed up! A large audience gathered as we waited anxiously for the acts to appear. Well, nobody came. It was deeply humiliating when I had to announce a cancellation. Naturally, we refunded all the patrons' money."

Sid explained that another house had bribed and stolen Sid's acts away from him. "But the next morning," he continued, "I scurried around to see an agent who was an old friend of my father's, and quite influential. With his help we got another show together in a terrible hurry; it was even better than the first one. I operated the 125th Street house for three years, then sold it and returned to San Francisco to join my father, just in time for the earthquake and fire of 1906."

Sid had another New York venture in later years, but his reaction at that time was similar to his first visit. He wearied quickly of New York and returned to California, this time for good.

3

AMONG Sid Grauman's closest Hollywood friends was the prime silent screen comedian and creative genius Charlie Chaplin.

Sid's first meeting with Charlie took place in the San Francisco show business world of early 1911. At that time Chaplin and his colleague Stan Laurel were both touring with the English impresario Karno's *Wow-Wows*, a lightweight English music hall revue in which they were making their American touring debut.

Always the astute showman, Sid was quick to recognize Chaplin's astonishing talent and potential. Sid was deeply impressed with the way in which the young Chaplin could rise triumphantly above his mediocre material to enchant whole audiences with his endless comic invention---just as later he was able to jump into the lens of the camera. Chaplin could make patrons laugh so hard that many fell out of their seats in the uproar.

"If you ever decide to leave Karno," Sid told Charlie during Chaplin's San Francisco engagement, "I can always find ample backing at my own theaters for any kind of show you might want to create and stage. Just say the word, Charlie, and we're in business together."

Chaplin may have looked upon Sid's generous offer as mere flattery, something said in the heat of enthusiasm, unaware that Grauman was not a man who made idle promises, as so many impresarios did; Sid's word was as valid as a written contract.

It is fascinating to speculate on what might have happened if Chaplin had abruptly left the Karno tour and accepted Sid's offer. The combination of Grauman the master showman and Chaplin the rising comedian might have generated this a hit show of major proportions, and if they had taken this never-to-be show to New York, both of their lives might have been drastically affected by its success. Chaplin might not then have come to films as soon as he did, although he would have done so eventually. Sid might even have started to produce motion pictures starring Chaplin and become a film producer rather than a stage showman.

As it happened, however, the two men parted company for some years. They met again and renewed their friendship when both were working in Hollywood. Chaplin was then making his own pictures, and Sid began to exhibit them. Sid presented two of Charlie's most imaginative works to the public: *The Gold Rush* (at the Hollywood Egyptian Theater) and *The Circus* (at the Chinese Theater). Both films, naturally, were presented with two of Sid's most lavish Prologues.

In October 1915, the following news story appeared in *Motion Picture News* under the heading

LIVE WIRE EXHIBITORS:

"Sid Grauman, proprietor of the Empress Theater in San Francisco, gave a special midnight performance of the William Fox production of *The Soul of Broadway*, starring Valeska Suratt, on Saturday, October 16th. This performance was an invitational affair and several hundred guests were present. Music was furnished by an augmented orchestra, special souvenir programs were distributed, and refreshments were served."

Sid knew exactly how to court the public; it is probable that he himself made certain that *Motion Picture News* received a publicity sheet on his opening.

"Mr. Grauman has come to be recognized," the article continued, "as one of the liveliest exhibitors on the Pacific Coast. He is a firm believer in advertising and gives particular attention to electrical displays. During his showing of the William Fox production of *Sin,* featuring Theda Bara, Mr. Grauman used a six-deck, four-storied electrical display of 246 letters. More than 1,800 electrical globes were used in the display."

Sid was already being noticed in 1915, some time before he entered the Los Angeles exhibitors' field with his father.

Sid's initial flirtation with Los Angeles came when he went on the road with a touring stage play he had produced. Friends of his from Los Angeles suggested that the southern city was a far more fertile theatrical field than San Francisco. Sid had only to look around him, they said, to see that the growth of Los Angeles would one day rival the great cities of the East Coast. Although Sid was dubious, he did start to think in practical terms of opening a theater in southern California; not in Hollywood, which was largely undeveloped at the time, but in downtown Los Angeles where the concentration of theaters was heavy.

Upon Sid's return to San Francisco at the end of the tour, he held protracted discussions with his father about the wisdom of moving south. Sid explained that he had surveyed the scene carefully and estimated the possibilities of their success and was anxious to enter the competition. Sid felt certain that the only way a shrewd exhibitor could go in southern California was up, *if* he knew what he was doing. His track record had already proven that Sid was an unusually resourceful showman who could gauge the public's taste with uncanny accuracy.

Others had gone to Los Angeles and failed, D. J. argued. Why would the Graumans have any special luck down there? But Sid knew his own capabilities even better than his father did. The name by which Sid came to be known throughout the entertainment world—"Little Sunshine"—was no trivial appellation. His sunny, amiable, soft-spoken personality won immediate friends for him all his life. Even the gushy and powerful queen of cinema sob sisters, the Hearst syndicate's Louella O. Parsons, at one time the most widely read movie columnist in the world, never had a bad word to say about Sid. She eulogized him at his death as "a very quiet and simple man, slightly built, with a great shock of wavy, unruly hair, a gentle voice, possessed of an overwhelming generosity and endless talent, who made page one stories whenever he invited some movie king or queen to leave their footprints in the Chinese Theater's forecourt."

Sid's exceptional personality was as much a major factor in his success as was his keen, business-oriented professionalism. "As a theater genius," the *Hollywood Reporter* said in Sid's obituary, "few if any have ever equalled him."

Grauman quietly discovered many new stars for the picture business, and he was an invaluable aid to filmmakers as an exhibitor because of his Prologues. Jackie Coogan was discovered by Chaplin in a Sid Grauman Prologue in August of 1919.

Young Coogan was working because his mother, "Baby" Dolliver, had danced in San Francisco for the Graumans years earlier. Coogan's appearance was in a Prologue called "The 1920 Bathing Girl Revue," which ran in conjunction with Lila Lee in *The Daughter of the Wolf*. In addition to twenty-four bathing girls in handsome beach attire who represented different Los Angeles motion picture studios, the Prologue featured ten children from two to five years of age, who were also in bathing costumes. The Prologue opened with a film of ocean breakers "with orchestral traps suggesting the roar of the sea and the wide expanse of sand meeting the water line," *Motion Picture News* stated. This touch was another superb example of the attention to detail that Sid brought to every prologue he supervised. He was wonderfully adept at setting the exact mood with musical effects to put audiences in the right frame of mind for what followed.

"As the velvet curtain parted and disclosed this pleasant holiday scene," the article continued, "the stage lights gradually brightened and the little children, with a few of the girls, could be seen playing with pails and shovels in the sand. A great lighthouse loomed left. Then the scene changed; the screen went up to reveal a fashionable bathing pavilion, such as Newport or Palm Beach might have. The beautiful bathing girls were clustered around the veranda, the steps or the sands."

The stage darkened. "Then the center door of the pavilion was lighted and the first of the bathing girls stood outlined in the doorway. It was Miss Louise Fortune of the Lasky studios who did a model's turn about the stage to show off her costume. Each succeeding girl was announced by a lifesaver with a megaphone and did her turn as her name was called, finally doing a few dance steps as a climax."

The girls were rapturously received, but a three-year-old girl and the four-year-old boy who followed her were the outstanding hits of the revue. "Little Jackie Coogan, the four-year-old boy, gave a burlesque version of the 'shimmy' in his bathing suit and brought down the house." On the strength of this performance at Grauman's, little Jackie was signed to a year's film contract by Charlie Chaplin.

At the finale, all the girls formed a circle and danced through several attractive formations to the tune of "By the Sea." Without a doubt, this was the most elaborate and expensive semivaudeville show given at the Million Dollar since its opening. Approximately one thousand people were turned away from the midsummer matinees and fifteen hundred were turned away from all night performances every day of the run.

Other players like Myrna Loy began their careers in Grauman Prologues or as usherettes in his theaters. Sid sent Fatty Arbuckle to Hollywood from his San Jose theater.

None of these successes had yet happened, however, as Sid was persuading his father that the Grauman future lay in Los Angeles rather than in San Francisco. In 1928, Sid wrote an article on Hollywood and its famous theaters in which he discussed the area's rapid development.

What does the future hold for theater in Hollywood, cinema capital of the world? Perhaps I can best answer this from my own viewpoint by reviewing the history of my own activities in the center of entertainment production for at least half the world's millions. My attention was directed to Hollywood in the first place as an unexploited field for the showman. . . . The future of Hollywood is the future of California. It has the same climate and the supreme advantage of being the world's film center, despite many attempts to shear it of this glory by other ambitious communities and cities. . . . The fact that I am in the amusement business to stay and have centered my activities in Hollywood is the strongest evidence of my faith in the future of the community from the standpoint of my profession—lightening the burden of the toil-worn members of the human race who seek relaxation in opera chairs.

Sid went on to state that his personal view of success was simply giving the public the high-class product it demanded, regardless of competition or expense. "It's true that the public is getting more discriminating in their choice of amusements," Grauman wrote. The showman's responsibility, he felt, was to keep abreast of this development, or better still, to be light-years ahead of the public, wherever possible, and to set the style. So, whatever the arguments were that Sid put before his father during the years of World War I, they worked. D. J. agreed with Sid that they should consider the move to southern California and test their professional knowledge and ability there.

D. J. Grauman's health was not good during the war years, which gave Sid more leeway than he might otherwise have had in the partnership. Most of the negotiations that led to the Graumans' permanent move south were in Sid's hands.

Sid's contracts in southern California that he had made earlier served him well. These experts explained that in the past few years there had been dramatic changes in the central downtown Los Angeles business district. Formerly, all principal stores were located on South Broadway between First and Fifth streets. But the city was growing fast; it could only move out toward Seventh Street. Property owners in the older district were dismayed at the spread and sought some magnet to hold business interests at the lower end of Broadway.

Grauman soon met many Angelenos who shared this belief, among them Homer Laughlin, a prominent entrepreneur who was also a student of art and entertainment. (The venerable building that presently houses the Grand Central Market still bears his name.)

Laughlin's dream was to construct an exceptional office building and theater complex at Third and Broadway. The Stability Building Company was created to erect the complex. Sid Grauman came along at precisely the moment when Laughlin and his associates were looking for an imaginative director to develop the planned theater unit. It didn't take Laughlin long to realize that Sid was the ideal man to head such a project. After some negotiation, Sid and D. J. Grauman were appointed to organize and run the new theater in what was to be the Southern California Edison Company headquarters.

The combination of the Stability Building Company and the Graumans ultimately produced the illustrious Million Dollar Theater, perhaps America's finest picture house when it opened, and certainly the most palatial unit yet built west of Chicago. The Million Dollar contained many features that were entirely new to theater craft. Architecturally, it was an ornate though highly effective amalgamation of Spanish colonial design with Mauresque and Byzantine touches.

Eventually, a 12-story office structure rose on the lot at Third and Broadway with 115 feet of frontage on South Broadway and 65 feet on West Third Street. Behind the imposing and still-attractive facade of the tower building lay the auditorium, which was 106 feet long, 103 feet wide, with a balcony 70 feet long. On its main floor, 1,400 seats were installed, 950 in the balcony. Sight lines were carefully planned to allow maximum viewing for patrons. The upper promenade level was reached by two wide, richly carpeted stairways, located on either side of the balcony. A mezzanine floor serviced the balcony, with central and side entrances.

Engineer A. C. Martin was chosen to design and act as construction engineer for the new office building and theater. At once he began an exhaustive study of motion picture and legitimate houses throughout the country. By making personal field visits Martin learned the virtues and defects of these various auditoriums and determined from his survey what he must include or avoid in the Edison Building's auditorium design.

As a substitute for structural steel, Martin decided to rely wherever possible on reinforced concrete. An arch of this material, twelve feet wide

Interior of Grauman's Million Dollar Theater: proscenium and orchestra pit (1918).

Grauman's Million Dollar Theater in the Edison Building, Third and Broadway, Los Angeles (1918).

and three feet thick, was built across the auditorium about halfway between the balcony's lip and the auditorium's rear wall. The truss of this arch was supported by a tension member containing seventy one and one quarter inch steel bars. Six reinforced concrete cantilever trusses supported the balcony. Resting midway on the arch, the trusses were anchored to the rear auditorium wall. The top of the cantilevers were the framework for the balcony floor; the lower side of the trusses were the mezzanine floor's framework beneath the balcony.

During construction of the auditorium, the Los Angeles city building inspectors protested vociferously against the construction work. They called it "dangerous" and "unproven" and stoutly refused to accept the finished work until a thorough test of the entire balcony was made.

Sid Grauman suggested that a bold, dramatic test be made by Stability Building Company, so A. C. Martin loaded the balcony at the rate of 250 pounds per square foot, placing on it a total of 1,400,000 pounds of sand. Even with this immense load, the deflection of the center of the arch was only 3/16 inch. The deflection of the cantilevers at their extreme ends was the same measurement, which was about half that expected. This test satisfied not only the building inspectors but Homer Laughlin and the Edison Company as well. The inspectors passed the auditorium as exceeding building code standards.

While the offices of the new skyscraper were being finished and furnished, Sid Grauman was paying special attention to the motion picture projection room. Sid located the booth between the upper and lower bars of the cantilevers, a few feet from the front of the balcony, and in its exact center. This location placed the lenses of the projectors on a level with screen center. When the screen was properly hung at center-stage level, it was squarely in front of the projectors' lenses, and sixty-seven feet distant from them. The advantages of this location of the projector were multiple. Proper light at low amperage was then possible, giving an excellent, undistorted picture for every seat in the house. This in itself was an unprecedented innovation that was adopted by exhibitors throughout the West in a very short time.

Although Graumans' Theater—its original name—was to be used immediately as a movie theater, it was designed for large stage spectacles, spoken drama, and vaudeville. The proscenium arch was

40 by 40 feet, and the stage depth was 35 feet, running almost the full width of the auditorium, or 103 feet.

These construction statistics do not impress today as they did in 1918 when the theater was opened, but they were years ahead of their time. The acoustics of the auditorium, which were given special attention by Martin and Sid Grauman, were exceptional because of the oval shape of the house, which did not require partitions parallel to the stage. With well-planned exits, it was estimated that the theater could be emptied in an emergency in less than two minutes through ample side exit doors. The aisles were wide, and the lobby spaces were airy. On the mezzanine floor was a rotunda, with adjoining powder rooms for women and a smoking lounge for men.

Ventilation was a special concern. Installed by Munger and Munger, a Pasadena firm, the ventilating system was of the very latest design. Tempered air was ducted in from beneath the seats to rise and fill the main floor and balcony areas. Air was drawn out of the auditorium through the overhead dome. This method assured a steady circulation of fresh air in the theater at all times, whether it was heated in the winter or, in milder seasons, before smog, the same as the outside temperature. At that time, large-volume circulating refrigeration of the type found in modern air-conditioning systems was not available. But the Million Dollar Theater soon gained a wide reputation as the most comfortable house in southern California, largely as a result of Munger and Munger's ventilation system.

The California Glass and Paint Company was responsibile for the installation of handsome glass doors and theater windows along the entire front of the Edison Building. Backstage dressing rooms were fitted with fireproof doors, another theater innovation. The metal door coverings were airtight, which prevented the inner wood core from burning in case of a fire in the house.

With the exception of the opera chairs, Barker Brothers' department store furnished the carpeting, draperies, the main curtain, and lounge furniture for the auditorium. These furnishings were specially designed and executed for the theater by Barker artists.

Not only were many of the details of the auditorium fresh and startling conceptions, but Grauman also lavished special ingenuity on the stage equipment scenery, which was built under the supervision of the Edwin H. Flagg Scenic Company. The permanent curtain and setting were designed by William Lee Woollett, and the backdrop was the creation of F. M. DuMond.

Woollett's permanent stage set aimed at a complete atmosphere; it portrayed a Greek temple overlooking a vast, impersonal Bakst-like version of Death Valley, with the Funeral Mountains in the background, surmounted by a greenish yellow sky. Between the proscenium columns were hung richly colored draperies. The portico of the Greek temple was canopied in the same general tones as the curtain, and decorated with two winged figures depicting Good and Evil in midair conflict. Both Grauman and Woollett liked the heavy symbolism, which would be too rich for today's audiences. The general public always responded to Grauman's grandly atmospheric houses, even if they did not quite know why. A giant cyclorama curving around the Greek temple gave the impression of an infinite horizon; it was ninety feet wide and fifty feet high, said to be the largest ever built.

The main curtain was a study in grays with giant redwoods shown in profile. The idea behind the design, Sid told publicists, was to show that life on the physical plane is seen through a mist darkly, whereas the flames and figures of Creation are shown on the astral plane in which the real life forces are located. Even though mysticism pleased Sid enormously, it was lost on the general public and may even have been one of Sid's more subtle private jokes. In any case, the curtain and the other elaborate auditorium furnishings verified Sid's claim that the Million Dollar Theater was built with the sky as its financial limit, and with the determination that, whatever it cost, the theater had to be the finest possible cinema temple that money could create, perhaps the best anywhere in the world for its time.

At the premiere one publicist gushed shamelessly about the decor:

A glorious, glowing, magnificent magnet is the crimson curtain which lifts from the screen of this theatre of many marvels, drawing all eyes to the centre of attraction, the stage. The very *liveness* of the curtain keeps the thought of the spell that lies behind it uppermost in the mind of every guest. . . . A Parisian lampshade of a creation by Barker Brothers, it is fashioned of lustrous, sheeny silk, with inserts of silken gauze. A stenciled green Maltese cross is the motive of ornamentation. Color vibration is life—it brightens spirits, quickens pulses and make life seem infinitely worthwhile. As Grauman's flaming curtain lifts slowly, a border of dazzling brilliants shimmers and holds the eye. . . . The effect is stunning. . . .

The carpets of Grauman's "art temple" were daring in their color schemes; woven in Byzantine designs of bright hues, they were quite avant-garde for a movie house, and so thickly padded that no footfall could be heard throughout the auditorium. The furniture and the Italian paintings that hung on the lobby walls all served to create awe in patrons and carry them deliberately into another world. Not even the smallest aspect of any of Sid Grauman's distinguished theaters was ever casually chosen. Behind even the most insignificant light fixture lay Sid's shrewd concept of what that item would do to enhance the overall atmosphere of the house. The original colored commodes in the Chinese Theater rest rooms are just one of a hundred examples of strategic enrichment on Sid's part, and installed at a time when all commodes were a discreet, uniform white in public facilities.

One media source called the Million Dollar house "a temple of stone." This description characterized the theater as cold and forbidding, when, in truth, the combined effect of the carved Corinthian capitals, the ornate organ screen, the rugs, tapestries, niched bronze statues, the gorgeous central dome, and elaborate indirect house lighting softened and warmed the austere expanse of great stone walls that dominated the house, creating an atmosphere that was relaxed and intimate.

"The walls of the lobby, foyer and promenades," the writer continued,

as well as the massive columns at either side of the proscenium arch, and the six used in the permanent stage setting, are of a manufactured stone like travertine, the building material used in the construction of St. Peter's in Rome. It is an agglomerate of small fragmentary materials of volcanic origin compacted together by water from springs with lime content. The imitation travertine is created by a new process, recently utilized in the construction of Philadelphia's Pennsylvania Station.

The chairs are deep and rosy, with curved back and leather-upholstered spring cushions, the same as those used in automobiles. Each seat is 20 inches wide, and staggered so that each patron has a clear view of the stage.

Over the main entrance to the theater [but gone today] are large letters in travertine that

A studio portrait of master showman Sid Grauman, taken at the time of the opening of Grauman's Million Dollar Theater in 1918.

spell out the name of GRAUMAN. [Below this is a changeable marquee, which announces the current attraction in dark letters on a translucently lighted white background, not there in 1918.]

One of the most unusual installations at the new Million Dollar Theater was the Hansen seating device, which consisted of two diagrammatical house seating plans, one for the main floor and another for the balcony, in miniature electric lights, set into foyer cabinets. "Each light connects to a single seat," advised *Motion Picture News* of November 19, 1919, "and comes on whenever that seat is vacated, thus enabling floor managers and ushers to pinpoint every vacant seat in the theater at any given moment.

An extension of the device is being placed in the private office of Mr. Grauman so that he will know at all times the number of people in the theater.

The device is quite simple; it applies the telephone switchboard system to the seat. On each seat is a small spring, and when the seat is raised a connection is made and a light goes on in the indicator panel. Every fifth row in the indicator cabinet has green lights so that ushers or patrons can see immediately the exact location of an empty seat by row. The operation cost of the panel is negligible, as a transformer cuts down the electrical current to ten volts, the required amount for lighting cabinet equipment. The equipment may be installed after the auditorium's completion by using surface cables from the seat rows to the indicator panel. . . .

The Hansen device was not only a novelty; it was a practical application of electronics, and it made seating during peak show hours a simple matter.

The Hansen seating device is no longer active in many of the older theaters, but the Million Dollar Theater itself still operates on a daily basis under that name. It is presently the home of imported Mexican extravaganzas—often featuring Mexican television or film stars—and a variety of Spanish-language films.

Changes have dimmed the original luster of the venerable house. The dug-in orchestra pit originally went beyond the asbestos line, halfway back onstage. It was used that way until a stage fire caused the house to install a footlight trough in 1924 at the curtain line, which enlarged the stage. In 1925, the Metropolitan Theater's lobby chandelier in the Broadway entrance ceiling was taken down and installed as the ceiling masterpiece in the auditorium dome of the Million Dollar Theater. Greatly altered, the lobby of the Million Dollar was reduced to a height of one floor, and only the grand staircases remained.

Although the Edison Building complex is now appreciably dwarfed by the soaring glass and steel skyscrapers steadily rising nearby, distinguished traces of its past glory are still vividly evident in its ornate facade and its durable, though stained, appearance. If the exterior were steam-blasted, and the interior renovated, the Million Dollar Theater could easily become, as has the Bradbury Building directly across from it, a handsome national landmark of vintage distinction.

[NOTE: Since the above was written, plans are underway to restore the exterior of the Million Dollar Theater and the Edison Building's facade, as well as its office space, in disuse for many years.]

4

As the grand premiere date for the first Grauman theater in Los Angeles approached, the newspapers were filled with stories and ads proclaiming the cinema palace a masterpiece that would draw unprecedented crowds.

The Los Angeles *Times* of January 27, 1918, said,

> It has been the aim of architect, designer and the builders, as well as the Graumans [President D. J. and Managing Director Sid], to give Los Angeles the pictures it wants in such surroundings that the theater in its bizarre and rugged beauty shall in itself attract a permanent following. . . . This was also Sid's ambition in providing musical entertainment so far in advance of other exhibitors that his playhouse will certainly become a Los Angeles institution, which explains the symphony orchestra of 30 pieces [soon augmented to forty], the signing of a grand opera star for solo appearances, and the installation of a $20,000 [Wurlitzer Marimba] organ.

The popular Sunday Symphony Concerts, which were not inaugurated at morning performances until 1919, were followed by the first full show of the day. Although the original Wurlitzer organ was an impressive instrument, Grauman apparently felt that the popular Jesse Crawford deserved something better. The new Hope-Jones organ that re-placed the Wurlitzer was formally introduced to Million Dollar patrons by Crawford with a special holiday program of Christmas carols on December 23, 1918.

The new organ was the very latest in symphonic instruments, so a press release claimed. It possessed a full complement of reeds, brasses, diapasons, flutes, and strings. By means of a recent discovery, a contemporary piano could also be played through the organ console.

Because of the heavy advance publicity that the new Grauman theater drew, very few movie fans in Los Angeles were unaware that on Friday, February 1, 1918, the most elaborate motion picture house in the West would be formally opened to the public. On the day of the premiere thousands of eager patrons were lined up on Broadway, on Third and Fourth streets, and around on Hill, trying to gain admission to the house. Several thousands were turned away.

The theater's premiere was conducted with great ceremony. The lobby was crowded with scores of huge floral pieces that had been sent to the Graumans by friends both in and out of town. The lucky spectators with tickets were guided to their seats through aisles of flowers by pretty usherettes in specially designed, trousered cadet uniforms, under house illumination that was just bright enough to display the various wonders of the auditorium

Facade of Grauman's Million Dollar Theater at the time of its grand opening (1918).

yet not detract from the audience.

Promptly at the appointed hour, the outer proscenium curtains parted to reveal the Grauman Symphony Orchestra in the pit, and the curtained stage behind it. An audible wave of surprised delight swept through the house. Everyone had taken for granted that the false curtain was the true one and would open to reveal the stage proper. Then, under the direction of Rudolph G. Kopp, operatic and popular numbers were offered in overture, the two groups in spirited contrast to one another. Featured on the new Wurlitzer, organist Jesse Crawford also won plaudits for a medley of hit songs, and a Miss Lina Reggiani sang "Most Beautiful Bird" and other arias to rounds of hearty applause.

Sid Grauman had not yet introduced the Prologue in its full glory to his movie houses, but what those first night patrons saw and heard impressed them enormously and made them warmly receptive to the feature film that followed: William S. Hart in his latest epic from Artcraft, *The Silent Man*. A full symphony orchestra and innovative lighting in a sumptuous architectural setting both combined to impress the spectators. The feature was introduced in a novel manner. "The beautiful crimson and cream curtain rose," said *Motion Picture News*, "and out of the nightlike blackness of the stage appeared a gigantic bronze bust of William S. Hart in his make-up of the Western man. Theme of the incidental music [to the picture] was a new composition entitled 'Big Bill,' written as a special compliment to Sid Grauman by Victor Schertzinger, now a director of Thomas H. Ince Productions who formerly served this noted producer in preparing musical scores to be played with films."

The lights then dimmed, and the film commenced. When it was over, William S. Hart himself appeared onstage to wild applause and much foot stomping. In his familiar cowboy garb, the unassuming actor received the homage with a modest grin, then recited a short poem to his breathless audience, rounding that off with a few casual stories of his early Western days before he began to make motion pictures.

As would happen at most of the Grauman premieres, the audience was just as much a stellar attraction as the film—or in this case, the theater itself—and contained more than a few celebrities. Among the illustrious persons present were producers Jesse L. Lasky, Thomas H. Ince, Mack Sennett,

and Hal Roach; directors Cecil B. De Mille and D. W. Griffith; His Honor Los Angeles Mayor F. T. Woodman; Chief of Police John L. Butler; Mary Pickford and her brother Jack; Douglas Fairbanks; Charlie Chaplin and his leading lady Edna Purviance; Japanese movie villain Sessue Hayakawa; screen siren Mae Murray of the bee-stung lips; smiling Thomas Meighan; Dorothy Dalton; Franklyn and Dustin Farnum; Ruth Roland; handsome J. Warren Kerrigan; Roscoe "Fatty" Arbuckle; Enid Bennett; comedienne Constance Talmadge; Charles Ray; Mary Miles Minter; Henry B. Walthall; matinee idol Stuart Holmes; the ill-fated William Desmond; and Bryant Washburn, to name a few.

With his unfailing sense of diplomacy, Sid Grauman had invited as his special guests rival theater owners, business tycoons, and many personal friends. The occasion was a testament to Sid's genial personality, to his ingenuity and showmanship. The definitive sampling of the famous and near-famous who graced the auditorium that night would remain his lifelong friends.

Interviewed during the premiere, Sid declared that this was just the beginning of his Los Angeles tenure and he had many plans for expanding his programs. "The stage presentations will become closely associated with the motion pictures that we show," Sid told the interviewer. "We will try our utmost to blend live action to the film's theme." Grauman, the interviewer went on to observe, would surely have his future programs monitored with close interest by independent exhibitors the world over. Whatever the future might hold for Grauman, the writer concluded, no one could have been prouder of the Million Dollar Theater and its dazzling potential than Sid's parents, D. J. and Rosa, who sat in the glittering audience with wide smiles as the show climaxed in a final burst of pleased applause, as much to honor Sid as the new house. Clearly, the young showman had made his initial mark in the Los Angeles entertainment world and would be someone to reckon with as he developed.

At the time that the Million Dollar opened, the movie industry was having corporate growing pains. Grauman had a contract with Lasky to exhibit Paramount Pictures, but he still operated as an independent exhibitor who picked his features for their quality rather than their name brand. By 1922 the motion picture studios were beginning to realize that the big money lay in permanent outlets

William S. Hart and Dorothy Gish in *Sand*, a Paramount-Artcraft film.

for their product. In other words, they needed to own the theaters in which they exhibited their films, so they began to purchase theaters all across the country. This was the birth of the large theater chain corporations—Fox, Paramount, Warner Brothers, and United Artists.

When Sid Grauman unveiled the Egyptian Theater on Hollywood Boulevard in October 1922, he was still an independent exhibitor. He screened films from Fox, from Zukor and Lasky, and from MGM. At the opening of the huge Metropolitan Theater in downtown Los Angeles in January, 1923, Sid was in partnership with Paramount Pictures. He severed connections with the Metropolitan in 1925 and sold his interest to Paramount Publix Theaters, who changed the name of the theater to the Paramount. In June 1929, two years after it was built, Grauman leased the Chinese Theater to Fox West Coast Theaters. One wonders if this took place because Sid was unable to book freely. In any event, the first film under Fox West

Coast management was the MGM musical, *Hollywood Revue of 1929*, with Midnight Matinees a regular Saturday night feature. Rube Wolf led a massive jazz band of some seventy pieces onstage, and MGM stars frequently made personal appearances to a five-dollar reserved-seats-only audience.

During the 1920s the studios had become immensely powerful through the motion picture theater chains and their practice of exclusively "block-booking" films into their nationwide theaters. The situation could be compared to the thousands of franchise businesses operating in today's commercial world. An exhibitor needed the partnership of a large movie corporation before it could show films made by that company, just as today's franchise outlets cannot operate without the umbrella company's product.

From 1922 through 1929, Sid Grauman chalked up his greatest exhibitor's triumphs, running only the finest features produced in the Hollywood studios at his various deluxe houses. He was able to maintain this high-quality standard because of his personal connections with the major movie moguls and because his theaters with their popular Prologues were so outstanding that the studios were absolutely guaranteed top exposure for every feature they gave him. Sid's natural talent for garnering publicity throughout the nation whenever he opened a new film often made middling productions into commercial successes that played for months in his two long-run policy houses, the Egyptian and the Chinese. No one was more aware of Sid's ability than studio chiefs like Schenck, Lasky, Zukor, Louis B. Mayer, and Sam Goldwyn. With their stamp of approval Sid could generally pick and choose his features.

Sid opened the Chinese Theater in 1927, and almost immediately after the long-running *King of Kings* and the film that followed it—Douglas Fairbanks's *The Gaucho*—were shown there, Sid began to have difficulty in obtaining top products to exhibit. The big theater chains, firms like Fox, MGM, and Warner Brothers, were channeling all their finest films into their own outlets. California's Fox West Coast Theaters had its own first-run monopoly up and down the state. In San Francisco the cavernous, fabulously furnished Fox Theater on Market Street would open its doors before the end of the decade. Sid's competition in Los Angeles, the first-run Fox house for "road show" features, was the beautiful Carthay Circle Theater, with Prologues that were colorful but no real competition for Grauman's productions.

Sid was finally forced to become partners with Fox West Coast Theaters in order to operate the Chinese Theater successfully, selling off his interest in the Egyptian Theater. The Million Dollar Theater eventually went to Paramount Publix Corporation. Sid had many disagreements with the Fox West Coast organization over policy at the Chinese Theater and ultimately parted company with the chain operators.

About the only problems Sid ever had with his theaters was the competition given him by the monopoly of the corporate exhibitors. It is remarkable that he managed to maintain such singular eminence as an independent exhibitor for well over a decade in an increasingly cutthroat business, but he did, and without peer.

One of the keys to the Grauman success story was that Sid never rested on his laurels. He was a tireless innovator who was always searching for new ways to express his ideas. If a particular Prologue won special public favor and Sid wondered why, he would analyze its separate elements and try to improve upon the successful combination in his next production. He was a stickler for quality down to the smallest detail, and would spare no expense to achieve what he felt was the best that money and talent could offer. It was axiomatic that what pleased him would surely please his patrons, the general public, and he was almost never wrong. Certainly Sid was on target more often than the movie producers whose products he exhibited and generally enhanced, since he never relied on repetition.

With the showing of Douglas Fairbanks in *Headin' South* shortly after the Million Dollar Theater opened in 1918, Sid was already starting to create the kind of stage show that would become his professional signature. A group of Spanish dancers entertained in vivid costumes during the fifteen-minute prelude to the main feature, which was called "Songs of Old Castile." Director Rudolph Kopp performed a violin solo on the same bill, backed by the Grauman Symphony, with Jesse Crawford at the organ in a program of Spanish melodies. Regular admission prices were fifteen, twenty, and twenty-five cents.

The late February feature with Dorothy Dalton was *Flare-Up Sal*, a California Gold Rush drama. Grauman introduced a dance hall sequence set in an 1849 mining camp. What made the sequence so effective was subordinate actors from the film appearing live on the stage.

In March a Charles Ray film was preceded by the personal appearance of actress Marguerite de la Motte, billed as a protegee of ballerina Anna Pavlova. She performed "The Dance of Spring" and later "The Death of the Blue Heron" with special lighting and music. The *Examiner* noted: "Little Miss Motte does one classic dance and later in the approved formality of the true toe-dancer interprets a dying creature in flight."

By late March the orchestra had been enlarged, and on April 1, 1918, the first film version of Maeterlinck's *The Bluebird* opened at the Million Dollar. The *Examiner* cited the bill as "another well-rounded program. Sid Grauman is preceding the screen drama with a delightful prologue [this is the first mention of the term in Grauman lore] that includes fairies, child dancers, and a musical program of much interest. Little June Hovick [later to become actress June Havoc, sister of Gypsy Rose Lee], a diminutive 5-year-old dancer, is graceful and sophisticated in her remarkable toe-dancing, displaying much sang froid as she faces her audience and accepts her well-deserved plaudits."

An *Examiner* ad for the Million Dollar later in the month defined Sid's work: "This theater is the achievement of an aim in life. It is the product of a man's heart and soul. It is a work of art and in it are produced Works of Art. When it's at Grauman's, it's good. . . ." The publicist was absolutely right, as the box office receipts attested.

Grauman offered a lot of entertainment for the admission price. Patrons came to count on such programs as the one of April 29, 1918, with an overture by the orchestra, Bohm's "Tarantella," followed by a harp solo, and the Grauman Educational Weekly, scenic and news features compiled by Sid himself. Jesse Crawford offered a medley of wartime hits: "I'm Sorry I Made You Cry" and "Uncle Sammy, Take Care of My Girl." Next was Mack Sennett's latest comedy short, "Saucy Madeline," followed by the Anita Peters Wright's Rhythmic Dancers. Then came Grauman's Topical Weekly, a revue of important events compiled by Grauman, and finally the tenor Carlos Bravo in an aria from *Tosca*, topped off by Douglas Fairbanks in a wartime featurette called *Smashing the Kaiser*. The main feature was Adolph Zukor's *Tosca*, starring the noted stage actress, Pauline Frederick.

It is difficult to pinpoint the exact date of origin of the famous Grauman Prologue. Bits and fragments began to appear shortly after the Million Dollar premiere in February, 1918. But the first fully planned tie-in was probably the stage setting designed for the Charles Ray film, *The Claws of the Hun*. Prefacing the World War I propaganda picture were newsreel scenes of the European war—battles, trench warfare, hospital wounded, Red Cross nurses, marching troops. The Grauman Symphony Orchestra played somber and classical music throughout. Then Jesse Crawford entertained at the console of the Mighty Wurlitzer with a medley of war songs. Onstage Grauman presented a uniformed male chorus of six voices in a special setting that impressively duplicated the deck of a battleship, the U.S.S. *Cheyenne*. In later years, Grauman would never have let such an opportunity slip by without including a sea battle with skies aflame, a storm perhaps, and certainly a full company of dancers.

The following week, July 15, Dorothy Dalton appeared in *The Kaiser's Shadow*, which was more propaganda. The stage vignette, called "Facing the Enemy in True Army Fashion," graphically depicted a front-line battle trench with American soldiers preparing for an over-the-top assault under a sky filled with exploding artillery fire.

On July 22, Grauman presented Sessue Hayakawa in *The City of Dim Faces*. Hayakawa played the role of a Chinese-American in San Francisco. The stage was divided into three sections in a triptych arrangement. The main set was a San Francisco Chinatown street facade that rose realistically three floors above the stage, with entrances on both wing stages. The film's title was projected, and the curtains then opened to reveal the set. Twenty Chinese took part in the pantomimic action, which continued for several minutes, ending with a drum tattoo that called the faithful of Chinatown to worship in the central building. Primitive, perhaps, but highly effective; public response was excellent.

A week later Grauman presented the long-awaited *Uncle Tom's Cabin*, starring Marguerite Clark in both the Topsy and Little Eva roles. The brief Prologue was advertised as "Fifteen Jubilee Singers in a Plantation Setting." In August, William S. Hart appeared in the sea saga *Shark Monroe*. Grauman staged a thematic prelude entitled "Sailing Schooner 'The Gull,'" which was well received. At the end of August, Pauline Frederick was back, this time in *Fedora*, a melodrama based on the same material from which composer Giordano drew inspiration for his opera. In a special set copied from the film, tenor Carlos Bravo sang an aria from the opera.

The following week Dorothy Dalton appeared in *Green Eyes*. The military theme of the stage show opened with a Crawford organ arrangement of the song, "We Don't Want the Bacon, What We Want Is a Piece of the Rhine." The footlight attraction was Grauman's Military Minstrel Jubilee, which featured singing actors costumed to represent the Allied Nations at war, in a minstrel format. The idea won loud public appraisal and highly favorable mention in the press.

Grauman held over the Military Minstrel Jubilee for a second week so that the journalists who might have missed it, and the general public, could attend. One writer described the show as the most skillfully staged and inspiring patriotic piece yet seen in California during the Great War. An entire forest of live trees, twelve- to twenty-feet high, covered the stage background to simulate the richly wooded battlefronts "over there." The entrances to tents were clearly visible, said the writer, while here and there camouflaged cannons were glimpsed between the trees. Vocal selections—the national anthems and late war songs—were rendered by a talented male chorus in army uniforms. William S. Hart's latest, *Riddle Gawne*, played second in reception to the stage show.

On September 5, 1918, Sid introduced a new dimension to the Million Dollar Theater in the presentation of the film debut of Lila Lee with the star appearing in person for limited performances. The film was *The Cruise of the Make Believers*, but the important event was the appearance of Miss Lee in person. "A breath of verdant meadows from the Sunny South, redolent of Spring," one critic rhapsodized,

> Miss Lee made not only her photoplay premiere at Grauman's but will be seen in person during the week. She entertains the audience with songs which are responsible for her being called the "phenomenon of vaudeville" without question. An unusual feature is an original setting created by Sid Grauman which shows the interior of a Red Cross hospital just behind the lines—*Twenty Minutes in a Military Hospital with Red Cross Nurses*. Two rows of cots are shown with recuperating soldiers and attending nurses. Actors entertain the wounded with talent. Jesse Crawford plays "For Your Boy and My Boy" with great effect.

It didn't take Grauman long to discover the public's positive appetite for realistic stage settings. No one was using the term "multimedia" in those days, but Grauman understood this technique and made one medium complement the other. His attention to authenticity in his settings tied the Prologues effectively to the ensuing films by dramatic contrast.

The 1919 *Motion Picture News* essay on Sid's striking Prologue to Charles Ray's *Hay Foot, Straw Foot* called it highly artistic:

> The stage setting used to provide atmosphere

for the presentation of a feature photoplay and to give audiences something a little unusual to see and talk about continues to thrive, especially in the West, where the art of presenting pictures seems to be some months, if not years, ahead of the East. The storefront setting Grauman has built is so faithfully constructed that many plays on the legitimate boards would welcome it. The setting occupied the full proscenium opening at Grauman's and every little detail was carried out to make the scene realistic. Baled hay used is real full-sized hay. The branches of trees projected up from behind a fence at either side of the building, of the sort that Tom Sawyer might have been asked to whitewash. Then there are the bags of grain, the two-wheeled truck used to cart hay bales and bags of grain, not to mention the shovel, fork and lantern which are added to give realism. Even the old log chain flung carelessly over the fence has been remembered. If you were born and bred in the country, as lots of us were, or spend your vacations far from the hustle and bustle of the big cities, you can imagine what a hit this bit of bygone days, for many Los Angeles people, made with the patrons of Grauman's Million Dollar.

Mr. Grauman did not stop with just the bare stage setting. He got all the realism he could out of his efforts. Two stray cats were induced to busy themselves in and about the baled hay hunting for mice, and perhaps finding some, while special lighting effects were used to give the lingering glow of summer twilight. The orchestra played appropriate mood music as the curtain parted on the fadeout of the previous number which had prepared the audience for what was coming. After people had been given time to fully appreciate the rustic setting for itself, and perhaps to catch a fleeting glimpse of the dinner-searching cats, which of course could not be depended upon to give the "same" act every performance, two children, barefooted and dressed as we are wont to picture the happy carefree youngsters of the country dressed, performed the "Hay Foot, Straw Foot" dance to lively orchestral accompaniment.

Not only did this stage setting give the Ray picture a dramatic send off, but much extra business was directly attributed to it, caused by the talk the setting made, and also from the interest that there always is in a good rural picture presented by a competent actor.

Clearly, Grauman's Prologues were being taken at least as seriously as the movies to which they were linked.

Besides the realistic atmosphere and the wonderful lighting effects, Grauman leaned strongly on music to reinforce the moods that he was trying to create in the Prologues before each film. When Enrico Caruso made his screen debut in December 1918 at the Million Dollar Theater in *My Cousin*, Sid prefaced the film with a chorus of twenty mixed voices singing in an Italian street scene set. One newspaper said, "An important feature this week is the prologue. It reflects Little Italy with the organ man, the Lucia Sextette, and everything, that is, except the garlic bulb. Sid has devoted much time to the installation of beautifully colored lights with which he appeals to his patrons' emotions. The condensed grand opera is staged with careful attention, so that the audience is transported willy nilly right into the atmosphere in which poor 'Mario' loved and fought for the girl of his heart. One of the favorite Caruso records carries the golden voice with remarkable clarity throughout the theater." This was the first time that Grauman used recorded music in a Prologue. It was probably also the first time that this multimedia effect had been presented on any Western stage.

In December 1918, Sid announced plans for another larger cinema palace to be built in downtown Los Angeles. The exact location for this theater was not named because of pending negotiations for the property, but Sid did say that the house would be constructed to permit any type of stage production to be presented there from plays to grand opera, just in case the popularity of motion pictures should decline in the future. The building was to be of Class A construction, with a steel framework with reinforced concrete walls and accessibility to the main city tram lines.

The last movie of the Million Dollar's 1918 operation was Cecil B. De Mille's production of *The Squaw Man*, followed in January 1919 by *The Silver King*, with William Faversham. the *Examiner* observed: "A dramatic voice [in the Prologue] declaims the introduction of the players and cleverly arranged lights give this scene almost the effect of 'flash drama.' A male trio brought down the house with a sentimental rendition of Carrie Jacobs Bond's 'A Perfect Day.' "

Sid began 1919 with a parade of Prologues to the various weekly bills he presented. It was perhaps his most fecund creative period, which offered many challenges and much to be learned. The public remained faithful to his innovations, flocking to the Million Dollar Theater and making

it one of the most popular attractions in Los Angeles, and beyond.

By October 1919, Sid was offering "a bill of tremendous proportions" with Maurice Tourneur's *The Life Line*, and a Prologue ballet "Unveiling the Temple of Love" by H. S. Linne, as his two headline attractions. "Dancing is always an appealing contrast to the less vital celluloid," said a news review, "and a vivid array of men and women in Oriental costume prove their skill in pantomime and the terpsichorean art in this elaborate spectacle. Lighting of special beauty is provided, costumes are in chromatic tones, and the graceful girls provide background to the three principals whose love scene is the dramatic finale. . . ."

Many Million Dollar patrons wondered how Sid could maintain his high standards week after week. It wasn't easy to do this and Sid worked hard on the Prologues. An interviewer in 1925 commented on Grauman's ability to coordinate disparate musical and scenic elements of a Prologue into an integrated whole that appeared absolutely seamless and right:

How does he do it? Like Topsy, his ideas just grow. Grauman himself cannot tell you by what system he evolves the sequences of his entertainments, and how he creates and then places the panorama, dance ensemble music, orchestral numbers, vocal solos, exotic attire, and the spectacle of lights. The technique is buried in mystery. A rehearsal, perhaps, might tell you . . . . It might, but it doesn't. From a thousand unexpected sources come the men and women who people the stage. They dance, sing, act, wield sabre and broadsword, contort or cavort. But halfway back in the big empty theater sits young Grauman. Watching, judging, he calls to the organist some slight direction. The orchestra leader catches from Grauman's lips a bit of melody hummed softly—"Tell that girl to come on from the center entrance. . . ."

So goes a rehearsal. Details, details. All night long it continues. Grauman doesn't sleep nights, only days. Processes of elimination, suggestion, addition, are repeated again and again. The form of a show begins to take shape. The abstract parts slowly start to develop meaning and life. Presently, subtly, the intangible has become a composite of art and beauty.

"But," admits Grauman, "while I try to offer a finished prologue to my first-night audience, it is a fact that I watch and work over this feature of the show for several days after the opening. First nighters have the thrill of being just that— first nighters. Actually, the completed polished performance isn't possible until five or six days have passed. New ideas keep coming to me all the time. I find that an act needs trimming, another costume of rarer beauty must replace the one we're using, or a dancer of great skill must be substituted for one perhaps not as skilled. And finally the performance seems right to me, so I can rest until I get ideas about the next picture for the house, when the process begins all over again." [Which meant that Sid was constantly at work on some Prologue, present or future.]

Sid has a wonderful memory which serves him well for musical phrases. His orchestra leader and organist are quick to discover the actual selection from which Sid may hum but a brief fragment. He remembers acts seen in vaudeville as far back as his days of The Unique Theater in San Francisco, and he will go to any lengths to recruit what he wants. When he conceived the idea of having real Indians in his prologue for The Covered Wagon [at the Egyptian, April 1923], it was of no concern to Sid that he had to secure special permission from the Department of the Interior in Washington and was obliged to build a special village so that the Indians could live as they do on their reservation during the prologue engagement. . . . No task is too great if it adds to the substance of a prologue. Grauman moves in a world of his own at this time and is never disturbed by the business details of the theater. In fact he feeds on the solution of theatrical puzzles. He concentrates totally on the demands of each new prologue, changing sequences until the fluid, chaotic medium has evolved in sometimes as little as 48 hectic hours into a spectacle to delight children of all ages from six to sixty, and which vastly enhances the action and pictorial values of the motion picture it accompanies. . . .

Science had all but wiped out the old-fashioned magician by that time, but one master magician still reigned in the Los Angeles theater world from 1918 through the 1920s—Sid himself. Sid probably never thought of himself as a superlative improvisateur with magic in his fingertips, but he surely was. Few show business professionals in the United States at Sid's zenith of creativity would deny him the title of Master Magician of Stageland, the man who simply wafted his wand over his domain of creative ideas to bring them brilliantly to life for the delight of all patrons.

Live theater today owes a debt to Sid Grauman, who dared to use ideas that even Flo Ziegfeld wouldn't touch. Sid could take the tawdriest prem-

ise and develop it into an object of beauty and quality. He did this not once but hundreds of times, from the Million Dollar Theater to the Chinese Theater, and even if some of his presentations were less than perfect, they were always unusual. Sid was a true theatrical phenomenon who gave great distinction to the exhibitor's art and set standards throughout the nation.

By 1925, the Million Dollar Theater was eclipsed by the splendor of the Egyptian Theater, but an occasional glittering premiere still drew crowds of celebrities to the downtown house. At the celebration of her eightieth birthday in April 1979, silent screen superstar Gloria Swanson recalled the premiere of her Paramount movie *Madam Sans Gene*, for which she agreed to make a personal appearance on April 14, 1925, fifty-four years earlier, while Grauman still managed the house.

"It happened," said Swanson, "that I had just returned in the spring of 1925 from France as the bride of Henri de la Falaise. Not only had the prodigal returned to California, Cinderella had married her prince. Henri and I were invited to the premiere of my latest film. . . . We made it a point to enter the theater after the lights went down, but as we came down the aisle, the lights blazed on, there was a standing ovation, and everyone sang "Home Sweet Home." I was seated between Cecil De Mille and Mack Sennett, which was appropriate, since they both figured prominently in my career. But Henri and I had to leave early to avoid being crushed in a riot of fans. And on the drive back to Beverly Hills, a long way then, I must have looked pensive, for someone said, "How can you be sad, Gloria, after what happened tonight?" Well, I wasn't sad, I was thinking how the audience had applauded me, not a character or a performance. It was an ovation for a personality. And I thought, well, I'm up the ladder, where do I go from here? That moment was the greatest and could never be repeated, and I knew it. It was no great surprise to me when I went East to start other things. It was Sid Grauman who arranged that important occasion. . . ."

Colleen Moore, in her memoir *Silent Star*, reports on the same premiere:

In France, Gloria Swanson met and married Henri Marquis de la Falaise Courdray. . . . The pictures in the newspapers showed him to be very handsome, and we were all anxious to get a good look at him. We soon got that chance. A

48

Gloria Swanson as Salome in a publicity shot for Paramount Pictures.

gala preview of *Madame Sans Gene*, Gloria's latest, was held in Grauman's Million Dollar Theater in downtown Los Angeles. I was there. So was almost everybody else in Hollywood. The theater was jammed with the young and the beautiful, all in glittering formal attire.

Just before the lights dimmed, the orchestra struck up *The Marseillaise*. A spotlight was turned to the rear of the theater. There was Gloria in a shimmering white gown coming down the aisle on the arm of her handsome, titled husband. They looked like the king and queen of some mythical Balkan kingdom.

There were to be other premieres, but an item in the *Examiner* of July 12, 1925, stated that Frank J. Newman of Kansas City would assume managerial control of three big downtown Los Angeles picture houses, the Metropolitan, Rialto, and Million Dollar. Newman was replacing Albert A. Kaufman as director of the three houses showing Paramount pictures. A while afterwards newspaper ads would carry the Paramount-Publix Theaters banner. The Grauman name and style had as its sole remaining outlet the Egyptian Theater, then playing *The Gold Rush* with a Prologue that was almost as exciting as the Chaplin epic and featured an ice-skating ballet, Eskimos, the exquisite balloon dancer Lillian Powell, and a stunning dance hall set for the finale.

5

WHILE Sid Grauman helped some very talented performers along the path toward "the double F," fame and fortune, these exceptional folk also gave Grauman the distinction that he so constantly sought for his various houses. Sid was particularly lucky in his selection of organists. Among the many brilliant keyboard artists who graced his theaters, none achieved popular acclaim more quickly than young Jesse Crawford who came to the Million Dollar Theater when both Sid and young Crawford needed the exposure. Along with Crawford, one should also mention other Grauman organists: C. Sharpe Minor, the second artist during Crawford's reign, Milton Charles and Henry B. Murtagh of the later years, and Gaylord Carter.

Crawford, like many of Grauman's "finds," had a background that contributed considerably to his creative drive. At the age of six Crawford was placed by his widowed mother in a Seattle orphanage. By the time he was nine he was exploring music and learning to play the trumpet. Later he mastered counterpoint, musical arrangement, and composition entirely on his own. At the age of twelve Crawford learned the piano, and at the age of thirteen he left the orphanage to attend a Portland, Oregon, public school. When he was fourteen he got a job delivering groceries to help support his mother and joined the local musicians' union, starting to play at various functions with a three-piece orchestra: violin, drum, and Crawford himself at the piano. He was earning from fifteen dollars to eighteen dollars a week.

At the age of fifteen, Crawford joined a traveling show, playing one-night stands throughout the Northwest, until the company got stranded near Spokane where Jesse went to work as relief pianist in a honky-tonk nickelodeon. A year later he suddenly decided to play the pipe organ, so he got himself a job in a theater with a two-manual, seven-stop organ, the first he had ever touched. It was, as they say, love at first sight. The organ was undoubtedly Jesse's instrument, as patron response indicated, and he set out to master it with the determination to become the best of the popular organists. Not only was Crawford a consummate musician, he also had superb mechanical dexterity. It was not long before he could take apart and reassemble an entire theater organ, which was no mean feat. Later, the organ at the Paramount Theater in New York was built to his personal specifications.

From Spokane, Crawford moved to Seattle, then on to San Francisco, and finally down to Los Angeles and Grauman's Million Dollar Theater. Here in August 1918, young Jesse Crawford introduced a feature that harked back to his old nickelodeon days, community singing. This was during the run of *Uncle Tom's Cabin,* and Crawford presented a group of plantation songs: "My Old Kentucky Home," "Massa's in the Cold, Cold Ground," and

Grauman's Million Dollar Theater: stage and organ screens
(1975).

"Old Black Joe"—with the lyrics flashed on the screen, inviting the audience to sing along, which they did with great enthusiasm.

The Los Angeles *Times* of September 20, 1920, carried an item about musical director Arthur Kay (who replaced Rudolph Kopp) resigning from the Million Dollar staff.

> In view of the prominence that Kay has achieved in connection with the popular concerts at Grauman's Theater, the announcement of his leaving that institution made yesterday comes as a surprise to musical and picture followers as well.
>
> A difference of opinion arising between Sid Grauman and Mr. Kay over the musical presentation at the theater is given as the reason for Kay's resignation. He will make his final appearance as conductor of the orchestra next Sunday morning and will be succeeded by M. Guterson who has been in charge of music at the Liberty Theater in Portland.

Arthur Kay's resignation was followed by that of Jesse Crawford and Ted Le Berthen, publicity director of the Million Dollar Theater. Whatever the reasons for these resignations, which were rare enough at a Grauman house to elicit news coverage, they did not materially affect the careers of Sid Grauman or the other men involved. Arthur Kay went on to become a distinguished conductor and arranger. Grauman was quite firm in his musical ideas, and the rift was a case in which nobody backed down and the only way was out.

Jesse Crawford moved on to Chicago, and final-

ly to the Paramount Theater in New York. In the popular 78-rpm recording market of the 1920s and 1930s, Crawford's output of discs was impressive, making him the most recorded theater organist of his time. During his twenty-month stay at the Million Dollar Theater, Crawford brought great distinction to the Mighty Wurlitzer Marimba organ and great pleasure to Grauman's patrons.

The 1919 Sunday Morning Symphony Concerts began as organ recitals, given each Sunday from 11:15 to 11:45 a.m. before the regular show. Later these concerts were augmented to symphonic proportions. Where else could music buffs hear a seventy-five-man ensemble playing classical music and then stay on afterwards for the regular theatrical performance? *Moving Picture World* said, "Such a fine aggregation was not expected in a theater where the top prices are 35 cents in the evening and 25 cents at the matinees. It is wonderful how large orchestras are springing up all over the country. The musical influence for good has far-reaching possibilities. . . . We are delighted with the musical programs at Grauman's Million Dollar and take this belated opportunity to congratulate Sid Grauman for arranging such events and to wish him and Arthur Kay many more wonderful programs. . . ."

While the Sunday morning symphony concerts were drawing crowds, Sid was dreaming up many other publicity stunts. One of the most ingenious of these concerned the growing automotive industry, and the giant among them in 1919 was Ford. *Motion Picture News* reported on the event:

> Sid Grauman, one of the country's greatest showmen, staged an act at Grauman's Million Dollar Theater, in conjunction with his feature photoplay and program of nine parts that will no doubt be an interesting one for other exhibitors all over the beaten trail to read about . . . one of the most novel, unusual and appealing from the public's point of view that has ever come from the brain of an amusement promoter. The foundation for the stage presentation was the Ford automobile—the assembling of two Ford cars on the theater stage by two picked factory teams.
>
> The curtains were drawn and lying in perfect order, one on the extreme right of the stage, the other on the extreme left, were two Fords, completely torn down. On the one side appeared the blue team of six men, on the other the red team of as many brawny toilers. On a signal the two teams started. No faster

Grauman's Million Dollar Theater: view of organ screen and
balcony (1975).

Grauman's Million Dollar Theater: view of stage and organ screens (1975).

work has ever been seen, and the symphony orchestra assisted matters by playing rapid music, increasing the tempo as the two "tin lizzies" were put together. The hurried actions of the workmen, the quick music and the general state of excitement completely enwrapped the audience until finally when the task of assembling the two Ford cars was complete, the applause was thunderous. This novel act became the talk of the town. People thronged the Million Dollar from its opening morning show to the last show at night. It was also necessary to stage an extra late night show. The winning team was presented with a cash prize, as well as an elaborate pennant by Sid Grauman on the final night.

The local Ford assembly plant, which is the largest on the West Coast, grasped Mr. Grau-

man's suggestion at once, and also the rare opportunity to exhibit the Ford car from its component parts to its completed glory. For three days of the week Los Angeles streets were alive with Fords, Fords and more Fords, all on planned parade. The parade consisted of 300 new Fords from the factory, and 300 more individually and patriotically owned cars, all anxious to have the world know they owned Fords. Large banners announced the fact that the great assembling act was being given onstage at Grauman's. Never in the history of the photoplay theater had a stage presentation gone over with more startling a rush than did this act, and it is something that can be executed in any town at little or no expense, and with the full cooperation of the Ford agencies in the specified communities.

A week before the Ford extravaganza, Grauman presented D. W. Griffith's photoplay, *The Girl Who*

Stayed at Home. Griffith was a popular director, and the film was held over, so during the second week, to add some spice, Grauman showcased a dancing novelty, introducing Griffith's new and talented star, Clarine Seymour (known as Cutie Beautiful). Seymour appeared in a ballroom dancing act in New York's latest "craze-dance," the "London Tap Trot," in which the world-renowned dancer Rudolfo Di Valentina also made his appearance. The dance was one of Di Valentina's current original creations, and it took Los Angeles by storm. The male dancer was, of course, soon to become the screen's great male superstar Rudolph Valentino by his appearance in *The Four Horsemen of the Apocalypse.*

Five years later, on August 11, 1924, Grauman staged the world premiere of Valentino's latest film, the screen version of Booth Tarkington's enchanting novel *Monsieur Beaucaire.* The distinguished cast of this film included Bebe Daniels, Lois Wilson, Doris Kenyon, and Lowell Sherman, all sterling players. The flappers' idol in an offbeat baroque costume comedy-drama of stylish proportions was augmented on the Million Dollar stage by a sumptuous Prologue called *A Musicale at Madame Pompadour's,* which met with great popular response and was held over four more weeks to accommodate the large crowds, which were predominantly female.

The *Examiner* ran a special Sunday feature on March 9, 1924, to whet early interest in *Monsieur Beaucaire.* The article gushed: "HERE HE IS!

Louise Dresser and Rudolph Valentino in *The Eagle,* the story of Catherine the Great.

RUDY VALENTINO IN 'MONSIEUR BEAUCAIRE'! OH GIRLS! ISN'T HE JUST DEAR IN KNEE BREECHES? Surely it was quite time for Rudolph [or Rodolph, as he spelled it before his new contract] Valentino to return to the screen, when so captivating a part as this in 'Monsieur Beaucaire' was offered him after an absence of two years. He will have two beautiful leading ladies, Lois Wilson and Bebe Daniels. . . ."

Grauman had already started the buildup of publicity that would make Valentino's most sophisticated costume film known to his almost exclusively female audiences. Grauman knew that most men would not be attracted to the international hero in wigs, satins, and prominent beauty marks, anymore than they were to his earlier image as a desert sheikh.

As always Sid managed to balance the idolizing public's wide popular cinema passion with a little culture. An advertisement in the Los Angeles *Times* of January 1, 1921, attests to the continuing attraction of the Sunday Morning Symphony Concerts. The lines would begin to form early Sunday mornings down Broadway, for the public knew it could always count on light-to-serious symphonic music in a satisfying program at the Million Dollar Theater.

On New Year's morning of 1921, Sid presented the brilliant young coloratura soprano Mabelle Borch in a recital of operatic arias. An added feature was the Metropolitan Quartette, which also presented operatic selections. All seats were reserved at these concerts and were priced at fifty cents. The conductor at that time was Misha Guterson. Grauman patrons with long memories who talk of these concerts can often recall the entire program for a given Sunday, although the movie presented in conjunction seems dim by comparison, as even the Prologue often does.

In early October 1919, Sid Grauman took a breather and entrained for New York. While there he was entertained by fellow exhibitors and written up in *Motion Picture News:* "There is nothing upstage about Sid Grauman," the trade journal stated. "He meets you more than half way and acts as if he liked it. He is still a boy in his enthusiasm and it doesn't have to be a big thing to interest him. He talks well but is more than modest in what he says. Knowing New York, it is twelve years since he's visited it. He spoke easily of his theater ideals; he handed Famous Players Lasky and the assembled scribes some bouquets, then sat down to hear what others had to say. Sid Grauman has a smile that won't come off, but he is a very serious exhibitor."

Having impressed New York associates with what was happening on the stage of the Million Dollar Theater, Sid celebrated his return to Los Angeles by presenting a program that broke all previous records at his Los Angeles house, even with six performances a day. Sid invited Mack Sennett to bring his comic stars to the Million Dollar stage where they were to make an outrageous personal appearance in connection with the screening of Sennett's newest comedy, *Salome versus Shenandoah*. Sid called it "the most stupendous comedy production made by Mack Sennett since the dawn of motion pictures" in his newspaper ads. The film starred sparkling Phyllis Haver as Salome, Charlie Murray as King Herod, Charles (later to become Chester) Conklin as His Favorite, and the wondrously wall-eyed Ben Turpin as John.

Sid was not content to allow the comedians just to walk out on a cold stage, make a small speech, and then disappear. *Motion Picture News* reported that Grauman

framed a program feature of Ziegfeld magnitude. When the heavy drapes parted the scene was an Egyptian court, brilliantly lighted. The comics made their appearance in threes, all costumed as wood nymphs or oriental belles. Every circle around the stage added three more to the group of "classics," until a total of fifteen were dancing to the orchestra playing a "Cleopatra" theme. The Mack Sennett ballet contained all the well-known characters of the Sennett Paramount comedies, and it prepared the audience for what might be expected from the Sennett stars. On came Charles Murray, Ben Turpin and Charles Conklin in the make-up and costumes they wore in *Salome*.

The trio launched into a parody on "Cleopatra" written about recent local events. After that came another ballet dance by the fourteen warriors against gloom, and the sequence closed. The personal appearance number was given immediately following the showing of the Sennett-Paramount comedy.

The Wednesday after the bill opened, attendance at the Million Dollar gave every indication that the bill would be a record-breaking one. (This was three days after opening.) At 7:15 on Monday evening at the first evening show, the number of patrons holding tickets and waiting for admission exceeded the inside seating capacity of the house. The lobby, which had a standing capacity of one thousand five hundred, was overflowing, and before the first evening program was completed, a two-abreast line extending some six hundred feet down the block had formed.

Grauman gave solid reasons for the phenomenal attendance:

This week is one of special added features of unusual excellence, and we're extremely fortunate in being able to present four distinct novelties that are exciting the public's admiration. To begin with, the Paramount-Post scenic, "A Voice of Gladness," is the most beautiful depiction of nature in her most majestic aspect that I have ever seen. The subtitles are taken from William Cullen Bryant's "Thanatopsis" and enhance the sublimity of the pictured scenes. The big, fine spirit of this added feature begot an idea from somewhere in the remote corners of my consciousness, which finally found expression in my securing Gounod Romandy, the famed local violinist, to stand in the orchestral pit and render during the screening of this scene Gounod's "Meditation" from the opera "Thais." [Either the interviewer or Sid goofed on the name of the composer of *Thais*, who was Massenet, not Gounod.] The effect upon audiences [Sid continued] has been most inspiring and the applause at the finale tremendous. The singing of Fred de Bruin and Jack Van is far above the efforts of most motion picture carollers, and constitutes a second feature that's immensely pleasing to audiences.

The third special feature is the Sennett Sarcastic Ballet, fourteen men of all ridiculous shapes and sizes, who burlesque such dances as the aesthetic "Pipes of Pan," "Bachanalle," and others. They were carefully trained by Charlie Murray and elicit explosive outbursts of merriment. They appear in an epilogue to *Salome versus Shenandoah* and their appearance is preceded by three screen slide announcements to the effect that the public may expect exquisite dancers, each the physical embodiment of a poem, whose movements are like the subtle shadings of a Rembrandt painting! Of course, the "coup de grace" or the "piece de resistance" is in the fourth and most important special feature, the personal appearances of Ben Turpin, Charlie Murray and Charlie Conklin following the antics of the Sarcastic Ballet.

Once again, Sid Grauman knew exactly what he was doing.

While the public was still aching from laughter over the Mack Sennett ensemble, Sid turned to precision and pulchritude. His large staff of usherettes, adorably costumed in white trousers with shoes to match, flowing dark satin blouses with white butterfly neck bows, and velvet tams, were the core of the Prologue. Many considered "A Tour through Grauman's" to be the most original program that had been presented since the opening of the house.

The curtain opened on a dark stage. A spotlight revealed a young woman who sang an original verse, "I Am the Organ," followed by C. Sharpe Minor playing a selection on the Wurlitzer that fully demonstrated the volume, range, and special stops necessary to achieve orchestral effects on the big instrument.

Next came a young man in shirtsleeves who advanced to stage center and introduced himself in verse as the man who operates the moving picture machine, "The chap who throws those pictures on the screen. . . ." The stage darkened and a screen some six by eight feet dropped down from the flies. A motion picture projector was wheeled on, and the subject, "A Doll's House," bearing the Ford trademark, was briefly flashed on the screen.

Then a soprano stepped daintily from the wings to sing about the conductor, Arthur Kay, who, in turn, stepped onstage from the opposite wing and was spotlighted while he led the orchestra in a number to show its members' special skills. Following this, an electrician appeared in working clothes and sang about his duties. He then repaired to rear stage center and slid open an enormous door to reveal mammoth switchboards with the lighting keys that controlled the stage and auditorium. With the aid of an assistant, the electrician gave the audience a dramatic demonstration of the many lighting effects that were possible throughout the house.

Naturally, Sid saved the most predictably popular turn for his finale—a "tour" of the house usherettes. Prior to the opening of the Million Dollar Theater, Sid conceived the idea of dressing his usherettes in identical yet distinctive costumes, and the black and white ensembles afterwards became the Million Dollar's logo, copied around the country by many theaters. First, a single usherette appeared in a spotlight to sing a verse of introduction, "I'm a little usherette/Who's always there to meet you,/To light your pathway down the aisle,/And do my best to seat you. . ."

The first portion of the usherettes' number consisted of a quick dance by four of the girls, followed by a general ensemble march by four of the girls, followed by a grand staircase upstage center. A snappy parade drill was then executed by all sixty usherettes, the climax of the mini-musical comedy.

After the curtains closed on the usherettes' drill, they opened again immediately to reveal five small children, ranging from three to seven years, who stood at attention and smartly saluted the audience. As the house roared its approval, it was clear that Grauman could as easily have staged grand opera and made the audience revel in it.

Still stimulated by the encomiums gathered on his New York visit, Sid staged as his 1919 Christmas gift to the public a show that the daily papers and *Motion Picture News* called the most elaborate Yuletide specialty ever seen anywhere. The feature act was relevant to the season rather than to the feature film, Charles Ray's *Red Hot Dollars*, which had its own atmospheric song-specialty introduction: a blacksmith at his forge singing "My Little Grey Home in the West" in a virile baritone. The Christmas feature was entitled "Christmas Eve in a Toy Shop."

In the Prologue, the curtains parted on the wintry exterior of a toy store, with icicles on the window sills and snow on the stage floor. "The act opened with a policeman making his rounds, stopping to peer through the windows of the shop, after which he exits," *Motion Picture News* explained.

Next two ragged little street urchins make their entrance, gleefully running from window to window of the Toy Shop and going into ecstasies over the glimpses of dolls and toys the frosted panes reveal. Finally both become sleepy and the little girl lays down just in front of the shop door, while the boy takes off his coat and spreads it over her, to make her comfortable before he reclines beside her in sleep.

The house is darkened. When the lights come on again the scene is the interior of the Toy Shop. Mechanical dolls, a dozen or more, are standing in their boxes, arranged in a semi-circle. The sets contain the usual appointments encountered in a toy shop and puttering around among the mechanical dolls is the kindly old Toy Shop Keeper. The waifs enter and the Shop Keeper makes the dolls perform for them. Exceptionally clever children were engaged for this act. One costumed as a colonial belle dances a pretty minuet, while another whistles to orchestral accompaniment. A team of winter-clad little girls execute a Russian Dance, another a Scottish Hornpipe, and then a little fellow dressed as Bandmaster John Philip Sousa, whiskers and all, steps forward to lead the 40-piece orchestra in "The Vamp." As each of the dolls does its specialty, they are wound up in preparation by the Shop Keeper. Then the scene switches to the exterior again, during which time the house is darkened, and the waifs are discovered still asleep, the whole thing having been a dream. The policeman returns, awakening the children, and after giving them each a toy, the act closes as all exit with appropriate music. . . .

There is no record of the music that Sid suggested for the toy shop fantasy. One would imagine that he conscientiously bypassed the *Nutcracker Suite* in favor of something a bit less obvious. He was more innovator than cribber, so whatever musical themes were used they were doubtless effective.

During the week of January 12, 1920, Sid scored what *Motion Picture News* called

another distinct artistic triumph, a double one. . . . Sid is the one exhibitor who oftimes presents more than one unique act incidental to a program, as exemplified recently by his Toy Shop act and an Indian concert pianist, and on another by a Human Bird act and Blackwood's spectacle. . . . His most recent duo of achievements was to present "Living Paintings of the Old Masters," some of the greatest works of Rembrandt, Rubens and Van Dyck. The act opened to reveal the interior of a vast art gallery. Here and there were small paintings and etchings on the walls, while in the center, in a massive gold frame, were posed living characters, immovable and immobile as marble, seeming for all the world a part of the painting. In fact, the public was puzzled, remarks overheard indicating that Mr. Grauman was exhibiting some original masterpiece! Then the characters stepped out of the frame, which was immediately enclosed by purple drapes, and danced a number interpretative of the painting's theme. The usual beautiful shafts of colored light played upon the whirling dancers, so exquisitely an artistic background, the scene was truly enchanting. Each painting was a subject absolutely different from the one preceding, and just so, each dance differed. The applause following the final number was deafening. Grauman, whose swift strokes of genius have been commented upon many times in these columns, did it again. . . .

Drama editor Edwin Schallert of the Los Ange-

les *Times* was a man of wide experience and deep artistic sensibility. He lauded Grauman for his courage in presenting an obviously classical act to command the plaudits of a middle-class audience. Schallert said, "The act is prophetic of an era of artistic greatness in motion picture presentation."

Never content with his achievements, Grauman was always looking for new ideas. A man dropped by his office one afternoon and explained that he was managing a troupe of Maoris, the aboriginal New Zealanders, representing five cannibal tribes who performed war dances and canoe dances, in addition to singing native melodies. Sid auditioned them and decided that their fierce, fantastic dance appearances would be a novelty. Sid presented the act as follows: A Burton Holmes travelogue, *The Maoris of New Zealand*, cut to half its original length, was flashed on the screen. The audience accepted the scene, with the grotesquely carved wooden idols and tattooed cannibals as just another Grauman featurette. Then, as the picture irised out to a pinpoint, the screen raised in the dark without the audience being aware of it, and a spotlight irised in on the same scene, with Maori warriors shouting and singing, the women chanting weirdly. The effect was electric, and the cheers of the audience as the act finished proved Grauman's showmanship once more triumphant.

Outstanding Prologues for which Grauman continued to receive praise by press and audiences alike were to be a colorful feature of the Million Dollar Theater for many years to come. Among the Prologues that received the most acclaim was "A Midnight in a Forest," which featured a woodland scene with four girl whistlers in arrangements of birdcalls. For the film *The Kentuckians*, Sid set his Prologue in the waiting room of a railroad depot. Trains were called, and passengers were entertained by a piano and a "talking machine" brought center stage on which records were played to piano accompaniment. The Prologue for *What Every Woman Knows* had a double act, the first half of which presented a Chinese magician with atmospheric music seen performing for a slumming party in Chinatown. The second half was Madame Rose Hovick's two energetic little girls (later to be known as Gypsy Rose Lee and June Havoc) in revue, offering a distinct contrast to the other act. Another 1921 Prologue transplanted an entire orange grove with fruit-laden trees and a packing house onstage, Sid prefaced the scene with film-shots of groves, which showed methods of picking and handling. Once the audience was engrossed in the scene the curtain rose on four pretty girls, actually packers from the California Fruit Growers' Association, who staged a packing competition. Deft hands wrapped oranges in tissue paper, their nimble fingers flying faster and faster as the audience leaned forward in tense anticipation. By actual stopwatch time the winner of one of the staged contests packed a large crate in exactly three minutes and eleven seconds.

One of Sid's most unusual Prologues concerned horses and was staged in conjunction with the film engagement of *The Home Stretch*. Misha Guterson, the musical director of the Million Dollar by that time, was cast in a film short subject, with Douglas MacLean as the other star. Guterson was discovered in the act of leading his orchestra which he brings up to swelling chorus of violins, trombones, and flutes as Douglas MacLean arrives and interrupts the music. The picture was so timed that when Guterson left the scene MacLean took up the baton. Not knowing what to do with it, MacLean takes the advice of a violinist to wave the baton about, and finds that he can make pleasing sounds. He becomes quite animated. Jazz music gushes forth.

Grauman fitted sound to action, as though, said the press, the actor and conductor had been there on the stage in person. The novelty won high praise from audiences and critics alike, playing to packed houses, who attended as much to see Douglas MacLean in *The Home Stretch* as Grauman's witty and clever Prologue.

The Million Dollar Theater was truly the birthplace of the mature motion picture Prologue. Over the years of Sid's tenure the theater showcased literally hundreds of ideas, most of them Grauman's personal concepts developed with the aid of carefully chosen actors, musicians, and permanent theater staff members. Sid, of course, adapted many themes from theater through the ages, but there was never a time when he failed to add some elements that were uniquely his own to even the most pedestrian of subjects. The Grauman touch meant that the audience could always count on something special at any performance. Without this masterful originality—the ability to put his imprint on everything he did—Sid would have been merely another shrewd exhibitor. With it, he soon became famous throughout the United States and Europe as a master showman who ranked with the best.

6

SID'S great popular success with the Million Dollar Theater must have exceeded his wildest dreams. From relative obscurity on the Los Angeles theater scene (even though he and D. J. had some twenty-one years of San Francisco management behind them) to the dominant role in less than two years was a rapid climb. His quick rise had the whole entertainment world talking. Incidentally, the name Million Dollar was not added to that theater until 1922 when the newspaper advertisements began to list the Broadway house as Grauman's Million Dollar.

It was understandable that Sid felt truly qualified to expand his operations to include more theaters, and while he busied himself with the myriad details of the Million Dollar Theater, he was also shopping around for a strategically located property. It came to him in the autumn of 1919 when he purchased the Rialto Theater at the other end of Broadway from the Million Dollar Theater, between Eighth and Ninth streets, through a man named Quinn who was the theater's original 1916 builder and owner. The Rialto was never to be the spectacular enterprise that the Million Dollar was, but right from the start it did excellent business, obviously because of the Grauman name and promotion and the practical renovations that Sid made after he purchased the small house.

When Sid took over the Rialto it had a narrow access lobby with commercial stores on either side of its Broadway entrance. The low, two-story facade was made of white glazed brick. When the house was remodeled, Sid widened the lobby entrance and refinished the facade with stucco on the brick. A large banner sign extending the full width of the building was installed above the arched second-floor windows, just under the neo-Greek, Parthenon-like center pediment. High above the roof and on the top of the building was a gigantic electrical sign proclaiming GRAUMAN'S RIALTO, a star centered beneath the name of Grauman and a flickering candle on either side of the RIALTO. Below the marquee canopy were more illuminated signs. Although the theater was a small house, nobody walking along Broadway could miss it, day or night, with Grauman proclaiming his tenure in flashing lights.

On October 27, 1919, an item in the *Examiner* announced:

GRAUMAN PLANS REAL "BIJOU" THEATER. Sid Grauman announces the closing of his Rialto Theater [just purchased] for two weeks. At the end of that period he will present a veritable "Bijou" theater to his patrons with entirely new decorations, new upholstery, and a novel production policy. Satin-covered seats, the fragrance of flowers and beautiful music are included in the house plans. . . . The first of three films planned for exhibition in the theater are of such import that long runs are anticipated for each. Cecil B. De Mille's *Male and Female,*

Quinn's Rialto preparing for 1917 opening. Renamed Grauman's Rialto in 1919.

Created He Them will be the premiere bill on November 10th. . . . Music of an unusual nature will be under the charge of Gounod Romandy whose violin solo in the Million Dollar Prologue of "The Flower Girl's Dream" recently introduced him to the local stage. Mr. Grauman will expend much thought upon every detail of this beautiful little house.

The notation about expecting long runs at the Rialto Theater marked the beginning of that policy at the Rialto and presaged the system that Sid would employ at the Egyptian and Chinese theaters in the future. At the Rialto the policy was really necessary, since no major film that was touted with Grauman's crowd-drawing expertise could possibly accommodate all patrons in the single week's run that pictures usually had at the Million Dollar Theater.

Grauman spared no expense in the renovation of the Rialto. The details were planned by William Lee Woollett, who had been so prominent in the successful design of Grauman's Million Dollar Theater. The refurbished house was christened the New Rialto Theater. In replanning the house Woollett built a thrust platform stage, since there was no fly gallery or loft. The platform could hold from thirty to fifty people. Woollett also designed and built an orchestra pit, widened the exits that flanked either wing of the stage, and constructed basement dressing rooms and a green room for actors and musicians.

The Rialto seating arrangement was the coliseum or stadium type of construction—that is, one continuous raked spectator floor that rose from orchestra level to the height of a low balcony. All seats were reached through main floor aisles feeding into the auditorium from the lobby.

The New Rialto Theater opened on November 20, 1919, with *Male and Female*, as planned.

The film was the smash hit that Grauman had confidently expected it to be. According to publicity accounts the Rialto was "the most beautiful little theater in the world." Although such praise was extravagant, the Rialto Theater was as attractive as Grauman's vast ingenuity could make it, and was probably the most handsome small movie house in Southern California.

From its opening, the Rialto Theater drew good audiences, which spoke well for the choice of bills and the quality of the house. The Rialto was not only competing with the Million Dollar Theater, which was featuring Charles Ray in *Crooked Straight* with a spectacular sixty-person stage show, "The Revelation," it was also matched against other formidable attractions in downtown Los Angeles.

T. L. Tally was presenting Clara Kimball Young in *Eyes of Youth* at the Kinema Theater, along with the New Symphony Orchestra and organ solos, and a prologue called "Dream Star of the Orient," heavily ornamented with dancing girls, singers, and acrobats. At Clunes Auditorium, Fanchon and Marco's 1919 *Revue Deluxe* featured comedian Harry Hines and "30 of the world's most beautiful girls" parading their charms on an illuminated runway, spellbinding a large, predominantly male audience. Miller's California Theater was under the management of S. L. Rothaphel, later to become the impresario "Roxy" of New York fame. Rothaphel was in Los Angeles to promote the California Theater for Sam Goldwyn who had leased it as a showcase for his films.

A week before the opening of the New Rialto a news story appeared in the *Examiner* about the New California: "The theater is closed for five days this week while many improvements and changes are made to the interior and exterior of the big photoplay house. S. L. Rothaphel of New York has been commissioned by Samuel Goldwyn Company to take charge of the presentation here for an indefinite period. He promises to surprise the Los Angeles moving picture goers when the theater reopens . . . next Friday evening. Mr. Rothaphel is well known to the Los Angeles moving picture colony and deep interest attends his first venture on the Pacific Coast. He has chosen to exhibit Samuel Goldwyn's latest production, *Flame of the Desert*, starring Geraldine Farrar with Lou Tellegen in a Reginald Barker production. . . ." Along with the film were "specially staged and musically interpreted scenic and lighting effects," accompanied by an orchestra of forty musicians under the direction of Carli D. Elinor. There was also a chorus of voices with soloists, a digest of news, a Prizma color subject, a Mutt and Jeff cartoon, a Brigg comedy, and other novelties. Rothaphel's prices were twenty to thirty cents for matinees, loges thirty to fifty cents; and evenings, thirty to fifty cents, loges fifty and seventy-five cents including the war tax.

For the second week, Rothaphel presented Goldwyn's production of "the inimitable humorist and star of Ziegfeld Follies," Will Rogers, in *Almost a Husband*. This was presented with a special prelude of atmospheric stage scenes, assisted by the California Chorus. There was a digest of news, an innovative slow motion subject, and Harold Lloyd in his first two-reeler comedy, *Bumping into Broadway*.

A special notice advertised that Will Rogers would appear in person to entertain the patrons *once only* each evening at about 8:45 p.m. Jesse Crawford and the second organist, Arthur G. Shaw, jointly offered a "Southern Rhapsody" by Hosmer, and Mme. Constance Balfour, a soprano, sang the "Ave Maria" by Gounod, assisted by a lady cellist. Besides these numbers there was also a "Southern Fantasie" presented by the California Concert Orchestra and the California Chorus of Voices.

This detailed mention of the California's program is documented here to reveal just how much the new manager had borrowed from Sid Grauman. It is obvious from the density of the program items that Rothaphel was also trying to give Sid a fast race for his money, for the bill was undeniably an audience-grabbing one.

Competition, however, never really bothered Sid. He considered it a healthy situation that could only improve the general quality of programming all over Los Angeles. He once said that rivalry just made him work harder and try to be that much more creative. Sid was generous in his praise of his competitors, especially when they produced a really good show.

Not only was the California house a big draw at first, there were other stellar attractions: John Philip Sousa's Band at the Shrine Auditorium in late November and the Los Angeles Symphony Pop Concerts. But business was excellent at both Grauman houses. The De Mille film at the New Rialto Theater was provocative enough to draw crowds and settled down for a long run. In mid-January the "world's most beautiful little theater" presented Violet Heming in *Everywoman*.

Grauman was diligent about promoting his second theater and aimed at long engagements on every feature he exhibited. He searched tirelessly for ideas to publicize each film. The exploitation campaign devised by Sid for the second De Mille film at the Rialto, *Why Change Your Wife?*, in April 1920, was unusual even by Los Angeles standards where it was always open season on exploitation. Ideas tried out on the Coast usually went East, especially Grauman's publicity gimmicks, for Los Angeles was innovative.

Motion Picture News commented: The pre-release showing of *Why Change Your Wife?* at Grauman's Rialto has proven to be a great success, thanks to a number of things among which was a fine picture. . . . Before the opening, it was arranged with a number of automobile owners and an automobile distributing agency to carry a banner saying WHY CHANGE YOUR WIFE? *at Grauman's Rialto next Sunday*. This was for individually owned machines. The agency machines carried a banner with the following: WHY CHANGE YOUR WIFE? *when you can make her happy at Grauman's Rialto next Sunday*. A teaser campaign in the newspapers was carried for a three-day period reading WHY CHANGE YOUR WIFE? *the vital question of the day*. . . . This was followed by a three-day pre-opening ad: The vital question of WHY CHANGE YOUR WIFE? is answered in Cecil B. De Mille's Paramount Artcraft Picture this Sunday at Grauman's Rialto.

Sid selected black-and-white life-size portrait stills of the De Mille players from the production and had these blowups colored in oils by a skilled artist. Instead of being mounted in gilded wooden frames, the blowups were attached to floor easels, draped casually in swirls of velvet that blended harmoniously with the pictures' color schemes. Leading Broadway merchants were happy to give these vertical portraits prominent window space, for they drew crowds of pedestrians. In each case an announcement plaque identified the actors, picture, and the theater.

The five daily newspapers were also covered with display copy and special publicity stories. An essay contest handled through the Los Angeles *Evening Express* was dreamed up by Grauman on the title of *Why Change Your Wife?* The contest offered $250 in total prize awards, quite a sum at that time. First prize was $100, second prize $50, third prize $25, with five additional prizes of $10 each and five more at $5 each. Top winning essays were published at the end of the contest with the winners' names. "No personalities must be used," the *Express* advised, "and essays must not exceed 200 words. Only those essays which the editors consider exceptionally worthwhile may be printed each day while the contest is open."

The following day a two-column, two-inch-deep ad appeared in the *Evening Express* drama section announcing the $250 in prizes for the best essay on *Why Change Your Wife?*. The same copy appeared each day of the contest, along with one or more of the essays sent in by contestants. The space covered by these essays was usually a column and a half to two columns long. At the close of the contest, pictures of the first three prizewinners were run. The campaign elicited wide response from the *Express*'s readers, which was beneficial to the newspaper's circulation and to attendance at the Rialto Theater. The *Why Change Your Wife?* contest idea was attributed to Sid Grauman and was developed by his staff and Al Price, the exploitation expert with Famous Players-Lasky. With De Mille's stylish comedy starring the ubiquitous Gloria Swanson, romantic idol Thomas Meighan, and the pert Bebe Daniels, comedienne par excellence, the response to the show and contest was excellent.

The Rialto Theater played many hit movies under Grauman. One outstanding success was *When Knighthood Was in Flower*, a Hearst-Cosmopolitan picture with Marion Davies. The film was publicized by live actors who wore costumes from the film showcased in the outer Rialto lobby by *tableaux vivants*, which were so popular then on the stage and in big-top circuses. Another rousing box office hit was the sultry vamp Mae Murray in *The Right to Love*. Grauman occasionally transferred the simpler Million Dollar Prologues to the small Rialto stage, thus continuing a film that was already popular in his second house without having to produce a new stage concept. In those days Prologue buffs were known to follow favorite shows from one theater to the other, catching presentations that they had enjoyed at the Million Dollar Theater again next week at the Rialto, but with a new and different feature film.

To achieve the unbroken long-run Rialto policy,

On January 20, 1922, Sid Grauman celebrated the fourth anniversary of the opening of the Million Dollar Theater. "In the four years, during which the theater has been catering to the demand for high class, wholesome and entertaining picture presentations, Sid Grauman has come into worldwide prominence as a leading exhibitor in the United States," said the *Examiner*.

His services in this regard have been sought by theatrical corporations not only in the large cities of the United States, but in London. To the latter city, Sid Grauman was recently invited by a group of British capitalists planning a string of cinema theaters throughout the British Empire. As a builder of theaters, as exhibitor and showman, Mr. Grauman is known wherever motion picture flourishes. . . . Already Grauman's Million Dollar and Rialto attest to his successful career. Within three or four months Grauman's Metropolitan will open its doors, with a seating capacity of thirty-five hundred, the largest picture house in the West and one of the world's largest theaters. . . . To celebrate the Million Dollar anniversary there will be a special program and Prologue in which Mr. Grauman's ability as a producer of unique theatrical entertainment will once again be demonstrated. By a pleasing coincidence, the fourth anniversary of the Million Dollar opening falls within the date of the tenth anniversary of the founding of Paramount Pictures, the success of which has been closely identified with both Grauman houses. Though young in years, Sid is a pioneer in the motion picture industry and will this week receive the felicitations and congratulations of friends and patrons from all over the country on his continuing success.

Walter Hiers and his bride attend the world premiere of *Adam's Rib* at Grauman's Rialto Theater, escorted by Sid Grauman (1922).

Sid picked and exhibited only the most provocative pictures he could find. The films he selected were often more intimate and more romantic than the Million Dollar fare, and Sid paid his usual attention to creating the surrounding shows. The period from late 1919, when the Rialto house opened, through late 1922 was a busy time for Sid. He supervised both houses on his own, since D. J. Grauman had died in early May 1921, leaving Sid in complete control of the Grauman theatrical enterprises.

In 1924 the Rialto Theater was closed for renovations. "To the attractive little playhouse," said the *Examiner* in July of that year, "goes the singular honor of scoring more world premieres than any other theater in the world. It inaugurated the custom of making these events brilliant affairs with searchlights, film stars, social leaders, politicians, and industrial celebrities in attendance." And, of course, in the days when Sid was managing director of the Rialto, his own genial presence as host could always be counted on.

The Rialto Theater continues to operate today, although not as a first-run house. The house saw its best years under Sid's guiding hand. Certainly Sid must have known that the good old days of virtually no competition could not go on forever.

Grauman's Rialto Theater on South Broadway near Eighth in Los Angeles (1924).

By 1926 new theaters were beginning to open up in outlying commercial neighborhoods all over greater Los Angeles. These new houses were large, well-designed, and built to present film features with live stage shows.

For example, the Figueroa Theater, Fred Miller's large house at South Figueroa and Santa Barbara Avenue, was a magnet for patrons in that area. One of the biggest hits to play at the Figueroa was *The Sea Beast* with John Barrymore and Dolores Costello, the film version of Melville's *Moby Dick*, accompanied by an elaborate Prologue with a square-rigger onstage.

The West Coast Boulevard Theater opened at Washington and Vermont, and the West Coast Uptown opened at Tenth and Western. The West Coast Belmont had its Vermont Avenue premiere while Sid was constructing his second Hollywood house, the Chinese Theater, and as Fred Miller was building his beautiful Carthay Circle Theater in Carthay Center on the edge of Beverly Hills. These and many more fine theaters were popping up like

weeds in Hawthorne, in Inglewood, out on Wilshire at La Brea (the Ritz), at South Crenshaw and Slauson Avenue (the Mesa), the Redondo at Redondo Beach, the Wilshire at San Vincente and Wilshire, and the Highland at Pasadena Avenue and Avenue 56 in Highland Park. All of these new movie houses were constructed of reinforced concrete with full fly loft facilities to accommodate any type of stage show.

It is doubtful that all of these theaters would have been built if Sid Grauman had not shown what could be done with a first-class auditorium, good films, and attractive live entertainment which often made the films look a lot better than they were. Still, none of Sid's strong competition ever quite topped him. The press often called him a master showman, occasionally a genius, most frequently a shrewd exhibitor, but in fact, Sid Grauman was a mix of all these qualities and, in addition, possessed the most highly developed intuitive sense of what was right than almost any impresario of his era, including Flo Ziegfeld, Earl Carroll, George White, and the concert stage's Sol Hurok.

Publicity poster for *Conquered*, starring Gloria Swanson.

7

EIGHT months after the opening of the Million Dollar Theater, an item appeared in *Moving Picture World* about a new theater that Sid Grauman planned to build in the heart of downtown Los Angeles.

"According to an announcement made by Mr. Grauman," the September, 1918, issue declared, "plans are being drawn up for the structure, which will be the largest of its kind west of Chicago. The house will seat 3,500 persons and will be so constructed that it may be used for dramatic and musical stage productions in the event that motion pictures lose their present attraction for the public. Deals are now underway to procure a suitable site for the theater which must be easily accessible to all the main streetcar lines of the city."

Grauman fed the press further details about the proposed theater in late December, 1918, but he still would not divulge the exact site of the theater, a good publicity maneuver that kept the public guessing. Any theater in which Sid had a hand intrigued the public and was bound to become an auspicious house upon its opening. Sid's well-planned exposure made sure of that.

The house mentioned in those press releases became the enormous Metropolitan Theater, which had long been Sid's dream. The new theater was massively beautiful, remarkably well built and appointed, and its location was perfect—on the Sixth and Hill streets corner of Pershing Square, opposite the rising Biltmore Hotel.

A month before the news item about the proposed new theater appeared, the Graumans made an unusual announcement to the effect that Sid and his father would shortly incorporate as film producers. "A studio has been selected," the item said, "which will be used until a new plant can be erected and production begun in the near future. The two Graumans will be sole owners and sole financial backers of the concern which will be called The Grauman Feature Players Company. From four to six films will be made each year. . . ."

This project, to be reconsidered some years later when Sid was in business by himself, never got off the ground. But in September 1918, Sid said that "while he does not contemplate employing any particular big star, he intends to select the best screen talent procurable. He will lay particular stress on the director and the story making the star, instead of the star making the play. Timeliness will be the slogan of the company and the first production will have a war background. The Grauman films will be distributed on the States rights plan. . . ."

Grauman's Million Dollar Theatre in downtown Los Angeles
opened on 1 February 1918, with William S. Hart appearing
in person and on the screen in *The Silent Man*.

Sid Grauman's prologue for Martin Johnson's travel film
entitled *Cannibals of the South Seas* as presented at the
Million Dollar Theater, 19 January 1919.

The auditorium of Grauman's vast Metropolitan Theater in downtown Los Angeles, the largest theater in the city when it opened on 26 January 1923.

Sid Grauman's prologue of *Pioneer Days* was a pageant of the plains with "25 Indian Chiefs and Forty-Niners" onstage. The prologue and features, *The Covered Wagon*, premiered 10 April 1923 at the Egyptian in Hollywood.

Poster for Mary Pickford's silent film, *Rebecca of Sunnybrook Farm.*

Grauman's Chinese Theater opened in Hollywood on 18
May 1927, with the auspicious silent film, *King of Kings*,
and Sid Grauman's impressive prologue onstage.

**Interior of Grauman's Chinese, Hollywood, showing Sid's
private box seats on the mezzanine level at rear of the house.**

Gloria Swanson's hand and footprints made in 1927.

John Barrymore's foot and handprints and profile in the
Chinese Theater forecourt.

Sid Grauman's hand and footprints made 24 January 1946.

Rex Harrison's hand and footprints made August 1946.

Facade of the Chinese Theater, Hollywood, showing its
1981 look as the renamed Mann's Chinese Theater.

Corner view of Grauman's Metropolitan Theater (later renamed the Paramount) with its unique two-street entrances on Sixth and Hill Streets, Los Angeles (1925).

Although the new Metropolitan Theater project was initiated before the Egyptian Theater, the Metropolitan took far longer to complete. Occupying the site where the old Methodist Church stood on the northeast corner of Sixth and Hill streets, the Metropolitan Theater was completed and had its grand premiere on January 26, 1923. In the *Times*, Edward G. Leaf called the theater "a monument to the genius of the architect and the builder." The theater cost $3,000,000 and was considered by experts even before its completion as being unexcelled in beauty and construction by any other auditorium in the United States and Europe.

Since work on the Metropolitan had begun three years earlier, remarkable changes had taken place in the district surrounding Pershing Square. A block westward on Sixth Street the new Pacific Finance Building had gone up, and the Pacific Mutual Building at Sixth and Grand was completed. The block-long Biltmore Hotel was soon to open at Fifth and Olive streets. The location of the Metropolitan had caused the long delay in its erection, but the choice had been right.

Grauman pioneered Pershing Square as an exhibitor. Since construction had started on the Metropolitan, two of the city's finest theaters, the Pantages at Seventh and Hill and the new Hillstreet at Eighth and Hill, were erected. A new legitimate house would open as the Biltmore Theater behind the huge hotel across the park from the Metropolitan. The completed Metropolitan, then, stood at the very hub of the feverish new building that was taking place in Los Angeles's newest business district.

"From a structural standpoint," Leaf observed in the *Times*,

the new Metropolitan Theater is of unusual interest to all civic-minded contractors and builders operating throughout the country. Constructed entirely of reinforced concrete, the building possesses features which have been the subject of much comment. The great balcony, which seats 2000 people, is supported by the longest concrete girder ever built, 90 feet above the foundation level, with a clear span of 127 feet. Because of a new type of construction, the balcony and great supporting span were subjected to severe tests [as with the Million Dollar] during early stages. Nearly 2,000,000 pounds of weight, or more than seven times the combined weight of all patrons who will ever be seated in the balcony, were piled atop the span to make certain of its safety [as was done at the Million Dollar].

Other novelties were introduced in stage construction at the Metropolitan. "The entire front section of the stage, fourteen feet in depth, can be lowered out of sight by means of machinery," Leaf pointed out.

The entire orchestra can be lifted or dropped, and when cleared, the platform is an extension of the stage. A similar plan has been followed for the organ console, one of the world's largest. Backstage are 40 dressing rooms for prologue and musical performers, preview rooms, a large, well-equipped carpenter shop, electrical systems, motors to control elevators and curtains, a ventilating system installed at a cost of $115,000, with 51 motors. Through this system cool air circulates in summer, warm air in winter. The electrical switchboard was specially developed for the theater.

The building has a frontage of 155 feet on Sixth Street, and 247 feet on Hill. Both street frontages are occupied by shops, with the exception of the theater entrances. The Sixth Street side has been set back ten feet from the building line, giving an unusually broad approach beneath the large marquee. Architect Edwin Bergstrom designed the outer structure.

A certain curiosity for the "whys" and "hows" of things makes a trip behind the scenes at Grauman's New Metropolitan extremely interesting. Music in the theater, in order to effect a perfect performance, requires such synchrony between the music, the operator's booth and backstage lighting effects that an electrical device has been installed for this purpose. [This was the first West Coast application of what was to become in time the entirely preset, computer-run theater switchboard.]

Grauman's Metropolitan Theater: view of auditorium from stage (1923).

The organ is connected by cables to electrical relays and the pipes, thus enabling this magnificent instrument to be played while it is being raised from the pit. During solo organ performances a prearranged "program" for the colored spotlights, which are placed in the operator's booth, the stage wings, footlights, overhead stage and some 750 spots around the huge auditorium ceiling's "doily," plays on multi-colored objects, the mixing and mingling of these with the painted colors creating myriads of shades heretofore almost impossible to obtain.

[As to the outer building] foundations were laid to support a 13-story building, permitting the addition of seven more stories anytime the owners wish. The building houses 100 offices, many to be occupied by various theater officials. . . . The organ is a Hope-Jones Wurlitzer unit orchestra, built by James Nuttall, one of the most famous organ builders in the United States. The console has four manuals, an echo organ, ten large chambers arranged behind the fresco work in the theater's loft, above and be-

Grauman's Metropolitan Theater: proscenium and stage from balcony (1923).

hind the proscenium arch, where the pipes and electrical devices for operating the giant instrument are hidden—while motors and air chambers are located in the basement. . . .

Sid Grauman personally takes charge of all the Grauman orchestras, with the able assistance of musical chief M. G. Elsoff. . . . Henry Murtagh will be the Metropolitan organist, Ulderico Marcelli, orchestra leader-composer. . . .

Edwin Schallert of the *Times* covered the January 27, 1923, opening and described the proceedings as a spectacle of dazzling splendor:

"A huge crowd surged around the Sixth street entrance of the Metropolitan almost demanding admission," Schallert wrote. "One of the most brilliant assemblages of stars ever gathered for a premiere, Grauman's opened with . . . more excitement than any similar event in the history of the city. It had been heralded for months and the culmination brought 20,000 to 30,000 persons. . . . Crowds stretched from the entrance for a block each way. . . . It required the united force of both police and militia to hold them back. . . . The massive magnificence of the construction, the fountains of beautifully colored lights playing over the interior and the ensemble of settings and pictures, luring the eye ever toward the stage, all promised to excel Sid's past efforts."

The premiere, Schallert emphasized, was not glamorous in the usual sense. Prominent men made speeches, with a final tribute to Grauman, who acknowledged the praise briefly and cited his associates, pointing out that the theater must speak for itself to the public.

The master of ceremonies at the premiere was the distinguished character actor Theodore Roberts, who said that in such vast surroundings he felt about an inch high, the sentiment of many. Roberts introduced various stars who were present. Jackie Coogan, then nine, took a bow. Ruth Roland tripped on and kissed Grauman warmly, to a wave of applause. Other stars who did brief walkons were Richard Dix, Jack Holt, Larry Semon, Bryant Washburn, Antonio Moreno, Hobart Bosworth, Douglas MacLean, and Bull Montana. Bull's appearance as himself instead of as one of the hideous creatures he usually portrayed on the screen was roundly applauded, especially when he concluded with the observation, "I never see such a big theater in my life!"

The stage spectacle, as to be expected in a Grau-

man house, was displayed with superb lighting. In the "most magnificent theater edifice in history" the stage show began with Henry Murtagh at "the

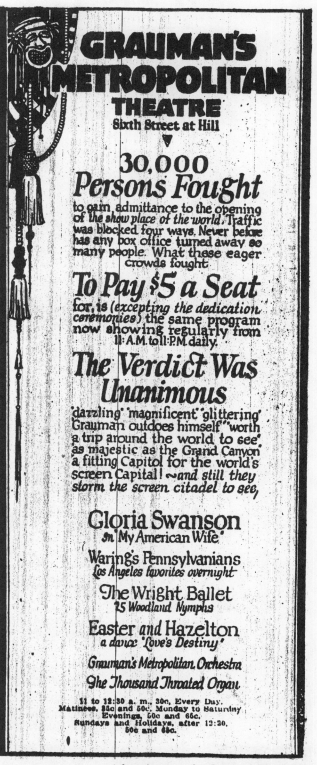

Advertisement for January 27, 1923.

Advertisement for January 26, 1923.

thousand-throated organ," followed by Grauman's Metropolitan Orchestra with Marcelli conducting.

Especially striking was the trumpet prelude, performed by ten musicians to the Grand March from Wagner's opera *Tannhauser*, which served as the orchestral overture. The ensemble followed with a rousing rendition of the Sibelius tone poem *Finlandia* and featured 100 musicians with a massed, robed choir onstage.

Next came the Anita Peters Wright Ballet Company presenting a sequence with twenty-five woodland nymphs cavorting gracefully in diaphanous gowns through a softly luminous forest glade of fantastic design and proportion.

Following this was the team of Easter and Hazelton, a fine dance specialty act who had introduced the "Merry Widow Waltz" in the original New York production of the show some years before. Their expert presentation called "Dancing That Speaks" included a revival of their former waltz hit enhanced by new choreography.

"One of the biggest novelties," said Schallert, "was Fred Waring's West Coast debut with his Pennsylvania Singing Syncopationists. These men, all college graduates, and all accomplished singers, each plays skillfully on one or more musical instru-

Gloria Swanson in *Manhandled*.

ments. This was the group's first public concert in the West, and their popular jazz arrangements were well-received." Schallert predicted a bright future for them.

Perhaps the biggest hand of the evening came at the very start of the festivities when the orchestra underscored the theater's dedication by rising from the depths of the pit while playing the "Star-Spangled Banner." On each side of the house, in boxes, appeared a figure of "Uncle Sam"—one was accompanied by a marine and a sailor, the other by a soldier and a Red Cross nurse.

The screen in the Metropolitan was placed as perfectly as the one at the Million Dollar Theater. Schallert said, "Never has a view of films been less sensible to eye strain. The softness of the silver sheet's disclosure is such that one is hardly conscious that he is looking at a motion picture."

The opening film at the Metropolitan was *My American Wife*, which starred Gloria Swanson and Antonio Moreno, and offered a Latin American atmosphere.

During the early part of the program, shouts could be heard from the crowd outside. At one time a group tried to push through the main entrance of the theater and signs of a riot were evident. But the mob was subdued by the militia, which forced the crowd back with rifles. Several times members of the crowd tried to take the rifles from the soldiers. The police were on guard, too, and were needed, so great was the passion of the crowd to catch a glimpse of the stars and the theater auditorium.

Schallert continued;

A critical survey of the opening performance can only take into account the permanent features of the show. In a way the opening presentation was a disappointment to those within the house who had paid their $5.00 sums for the privilege of being among those present, in that they did not witness as large a parade of stars as might be expected for such an occasion. . . . Several calls were issued from the stage for celebrities to come forth and present themselves, but most. . . remained stolidly in their seats. The group that did rise to the exigencies of the moment both literally and figuratively were chiefly men and the glitter of the screen luminaries' gowns were singularly absent. It was not the best possible evidence of good fellowship toward Mr. Grauman, in view of the magnificent domicile he has provided for films in the motion picture capital, but at the same time there was lacking some of that clever management in bringing the stars before the public that is usually observed. . . . Stars, like most other human beings, have to be urged to do things and one cannot exactly blame them for not . . . putting themselves on parade, unless a generous amount of verbal bouquets stimulate their interest. . . . It might, therefore, be remarked that the opening . . . could have been somewhat more dazzling. The principal talks of the evening were made by Judge Bledsoe and Jesse Lasky. . . of the Famous Players-Lasky Corporation . . . Musically, future presentations promise to be exceedingly alluring. The orchestra will exceed in size at least any that can be heard in film theaters in this locality. There is opportunity for real symphonic quality in the theater. Ulderico Marcelli has a chance to make a name for himself with such facilities as are provided him as conductor.

The stage is . . . of sufficient amplitude to permit large dancing acts. The one at the opening was in fact a revelation of finer and larger beauty. . . . A musical feature that was colossal in its spiritualized beauty was the ensemble of forty violins and eight harps. The "Ave Maria" was . . . warmly applauded. . . . Primarily . . . the Metropolitan is a theater for motion pictures. It will undoubtedly be one of the premier houses for films long after the industry had passed its everlasting infancy. Mr. Grauman has built for the future with an indomitable faith. He has a theater that will endure for several and perhaps many generations.

The Metropolitan Theater was demolished in 1960 to make room for a parking lot. So well built was the theater that the wrecking company went beyond its deadline and lost money on the demolition job.

Schallert's article dealt at length with the physical features of the Metropolitan Theater, calling it

ornate beyond anyone's conception. One gets the most striking effect by coming in through the main entrance on Sixth Street. Here all the massiveness of the mezzanine floor's decorative scheme strikes the vision. One gazes upon an elaborate blending of color on all sides and above finds that these assume shape in sculpture and fresco painting at every turn. . . . The building as a whole has a primitive . . . sweep. . . . The theater will be a glorious and perfect example of the palatial and magnificent that harks back to a medieval era and yet is filled with the spirit of the present day. . . . "My American Wife" is not the grand opening attraction one might be led to expect, but in the first few weeks the main interest will revolve around the theater itself. Gloria Swanson is one of the most favored film stars and . . . offers a resplendent presence in her beautiful gowns . . . Most of all, though, the public will want to see the theater and that it will flock there during the next few weeks, the mob surging around its doors last night gave ample evidence.

A year before the grand premiere of the Metropolitan, Sid Grauman discussed his reasons for musical programs with cinema in *Motion Picture News:*

When any exhibitor engages an orchestra to play every day and every evening in a picture theater and an orchestra of authentic symphonic proportions and quality to play every Sunday morning [said Grauman], he must have his reasons. When, in addition, he laboriously works on prologues, engaging talent and genius to participate as preluding entertainment agencies to the presentation of a feature picture, he must be convinced that the time and effort and money spent pays. All of which explains why my theaters devote so much attention to the musical program, not occasionally but week after week and month after month.

The problem of the picture exhibitor was to produce what Sid Grauman called "one hundred per cent entertainment. That is, entertainment that will give to 100% of his patronage their money's worth." Grauman pointed out that no picture yet made could do that on its own, nor could the usual vaudeville show or any musical program. A combination of all three elements, plus others, however, could do it.

"Let us say," Grauman went on,

Grauman's Metropolitan Theater being demolished in 1960. Onstage is Rube Wolf, orchestra leader for Fanchon and Marco revues in the 1930s.

Demolition of Grauman's Metropolitan Theater in 1960.

that your taste in pictures does not run to stories of adventure, but that you do like revelations of the elegancies, follies and foibles of society. You go to the cinema and perhaps you pay to see a picture by the greatest of all exponents of the adventurous and heroic in all screenland—Bill Hart. Your neighbors on all sides of you thrill to the well-told story, but you remain unmoved. The entertainment this far has been, let us say, 75 per cent perfect—it has hit the entertainment requirements of 75 per cent of the audience, but it has missed you. Yet on the bill is an act like that we are presenting this week at the Million Dollar in the engagement of Max Fischer and his "personality band" as an extra touch to a fashion show in which a stage full of feminine beauties display a quarter of a million dollars' worth of furs. You begin to feel that the

exhibitor has remembered that not everybody cares even for Bill Hart. Then jazz syncopation and social spectacle are succeeded by sublime music from an orchestra capable of playing anything from Beethoven to Victor Herbert or from Brahms and Schubert to Sullivan and Lehar. . . . You have enjoyed at least half the bill. The entertainment has been made 100% and nobody remains ungratified. It has all been worthy and on a high artistic plane. The wants of all have been consulted and gratified. Educational elements have not intruded themselves, but they have been present: esthetic taste has been excited and satisfied, and imagination has been consulted in a wholesome and healthy manner. . . . That is why Grauman's theaters will continue to serve every kind of taste except the coarse by a diversity of entertainment that is aimed week after week at the bullseye of "100 per cent" entertainment.

Hollywood historian Ben Hall in his book *The Best Remaining Seats* called the enormous Metropolitan Theater's raw concrete and primal color design Hispano-Persian. This probably comes as close as any description can to describing the polyglot splendor of the giant proscenium with its two side columns surmounted by mythical griffon heads, and the neo-Persepolis medallions which serve as ornaments on the peak of the proscenium arch. The fire curtain bore the legend, which was visible when the curtain hung in its final raised position, *Not by Might, Not by Power*, attesting to Sid's quietly religious faith. But Grauman was to come into his own architecturally with the Hollywood Egyptian and later the Chinese Theater. In those houses no one had to guess their artistic derivation; they were indisputably what their names implied.

Al Price wrote about the Metropolitan house from a preview of it for the *Examiner* on January 26:

The interior is like a Wagner symphony. Upon entering it vibrates through one's mentality like the breaking of a storm. It is shocking, mystifying, terrific in its power to magnetize; the first impulse is to turn and flee. But the character of it fascinates, and bids one to enter further. The effect is wonderful, and is brought about in part by the most phenomenal bit of lighting possible to obtain. The hard tile of the inner lobby floor is supplanted by the downy softness of luxurious rugs in which one sinks into what seems oblivion. Time and again one gazes at some stone figure, partly fawn, partly snail, then realizes that one hasn't been transported to another world but is still in this one.

The concrete form of the interior is the result of long study and planning on the part of Sid Grauman and architect William Lee Woollett. Edwin Bergstrom was the architect for the building proper.

Price went on to describe the molded-in-place con-

crete design, which was grander than any other movie house in the country..

As in the Million Dollar Theater, the sight lines for patrons at the Metropolitan were perfect, as were the acoustics. William Lee Woollett wrote in a by-line article in the January 26 *Examiner*:

In order to meet the specifications that Sid Grauman demanded, it was necessary for me to throw aside the rule of thumb methods which have characterized the solution of acoustic problems in theater construction for a half century in America, and go my way alone. I am pleased to say that now one can actually hear in the theater [there was no public address system], as one would in an out-of-door amphitheater.

It is commonly understood that the waiting room of the Pennsylvania Station in New York is the largest scale interior in the United States. This is true no longer. The Metropolitan auditorium was just as large. If the auditorium of the Million Dollar were placed inside the Metropolitan, there would be room between the roof of the smaller house and the roof of the larger for more than an average-sized bungalow court.

The house has not been seated to its capacity [which was 4,400]. That is to say, the city ordinances would allow a larger number of auditorium seats than have been installed. . . . Certain rows of seats have been eliminated to provide ample circulating areas. Like the Hippodrome in New York, this theater is provided with a platform for orchestras which raises and lowers at the touch of an electric button. An additional platform raises the organ console.

These facilities were then unique to motion picture houses as a combination feature, but not long afterwards they came into general use in many theaters in other large cities across the country.

Kenneth Taylor in the January 26 *Times* wrote about Woollett's use of concrete:

Inspect closely the construction of the house. You will be struck with the thought that the cement age is here at last; the material has been used almost exclusively. The great stone pillars on either side of the stage could be stone or marble, but they are not, they are wood. In fact, the entire stage is enclosed in a wooden shell which acts as a sounding board when the orchestra is heard in concert numbers. . . . Mr. Woollett's inspiration was to use concrete throughout the house above all other materials. The plush cloth covering the bases of the pillars appears to be plush, but it isn't, it's concrete and the pillars are merely painted to resemble cloth.

For the most part, the cement has been left unfinished. The walls are rough, revealing the grain of the boards used for molds. Edges of the material protrude where it has oozed out between those boards. Not only are the crude edges still left to view; they are emphasized with gold leaf. To sum it up—huge and massive it is. Beautiful and simple—and finely primitive. . .

The building that housed the Metropolitan Theater was not completed to its planned height. On August 20, 1921, in the middle of construction, a photo of the clay model of the $3 million structure was published in *Motion Picture News*. The accompanying article stated that two shifts of 800 men each were speeding up work on the Metropolitan to have it ready for its premiere on January 1, 1922, although the theater was not to open for another year. To speed up work on the theater, the contractors established offices on the work site. The original design included "height-limit" wings on either side of the auditorium and to its rear. These wings were never erected, probably because the $3 million budget could not be stretched to build floors more than half that height, or six stories.

The Los Angeles *Examiner* of January 21, 1923, stated that the building of the Metropolitan Theater cost approximately $4 million. The paper also stated that the seating capacity of the theater was 4,000. Whether it contained 3,500 seats or 4,000 as originally designed, the house was a mammoth construction with the longest concrete girder and truss system yet used in a theater to support the capacious balcony and roof. The organ was a Wurlitzer, the largest ever built. When the organ was played at full volume, the huge auditorium actually vibrated. Twelve large transformers introduced current to supply the vast lighting system and the numerous backstage motors that operated the curtains and scenery.

The concrete construction was not new, of course, but Woollett's use of it, as pointed out, was different and exciting. The overall design was drawn from Grecian, Roman, Egyptian, and Chinese influences to create a style that was entirely American, or more specifically, Graumanesque. The projection booth was 180 feet from the screen, the greatest distance in any theater on the West Coast, which indicates the huge size of the house.

The Metropolitan Theater was equipped with extensive lounges for men and women. On the mezzanine were a large candlestick, a mirror, and a Spanish room to attract patrons who were waiting for admission to the auditorium. The artists who did the finishing color touches to the house said that if patrons got bored with sitting in the balcony they could always amuse themselves by studying the intricate ceiling.

At the opening performance of the Metropolitan, patrons in the balcony and orchestra were busy looking at the celebrities who were present. A partial list included Adolph Zukor and other notables from the Famous Players-Lasky Corporation of New York; Mr. and Mrs. Jesse L. Lasky; Mrs. Cecil B. De Mille; Mr. and Mrs. William De Mille; Gloria Swanson and her mother; Sam Wood; Pola Negri; Antonio Moreno; Jeanie McPherson; Mr. and Mrs. Conrad Nagel; Mr. and Mrs. Jack Holt; Betty Compson; Agnes Ayres; Mary Miles Minter and her mother; Jerome Beatty; June Mathis; Mr. and Mrs. Jack Coogan and their son, Jackie; Mr. and Mrs. Buster Keaton; Joseph Schenck; Misses Norma and Constance Talmadge, and their mother, Peg Talmadge; Larry Semon; Sam Warner; Richard Dix; Helen Chandler; Claire Windsor and her mother; Ruth Roland; Hobart Bosworth; Paul Bern; Mr. and Mrs. Milton Sills; Priscilla Dean; Kathleen Clifford; Erich von Stroheim and Clara Kimball Young; Douglas Fairbanks and Mary Pickford; Mr. and Mrs. Charles Ray; Fred Niblo; Enid Bennett; Bert Lytell; Marshall Neilan; Blanche Sweet; Dorothy Phillips; Mr. and Mrs. Tom Mix; Alec Francis; Irving Thalberg; Harold Lloyd; Hal Roach; Mr. and Mrs. Hunt Stromberg; Charles Chaplin; Mr. and Mrs. Thomas Ince; Julia Faye; Marie Prevost; Mae Busch; J. Warren Kerrigan; Lois Wilson; Mr. and Mrs. William Desmond; Victor Schertzinger; Mr. and Mrs. Carter De Haven; Al Christie; Helen Ferguson; Jack White; Pauline Starke; and many, many others, including public officials, such as Governor and Mrs. Friend Richardson; Mayor and Mrs. Cryer; Mr. and Mrs. Homer Laughlin; and Mr. and Mrs. William Gibbs MacAdoo.

The Metropolitan Theater was never to present the elaborate Prologues that distinguished the Million Dollar, Egyptian, and Chinese theaters. The bill during the week of February 3 at the huge new house offered the continuing appearance of Fred Waring's Pennsylvanians, Frederick Easter and

Ruth Hazleton in a new dance fantasy, and the Wright Ballet, this time with the twenty-five nymphs cavorting in something called "Pastimes in Egypt," with the Metropolitan Symphony Orchestra and organist Henry Murtagh at the Wurlitzer. The feature film was *Back Home and Broke* with Thomas Meighan and Lila Lee. During the following week, Leatrice Joy, Raymond Hatton, and George Fawcett appeared in *Java Head*, with essentially the same stage artists in a different program.

On March 3, the bill changed to Marion Davies in *Adam and Eva*, with T. Roy Barnes. Onstage, Grauman presented the William Morris production of Jane and Katherine Lee in "The New Director," which was advertised as a famous comedy drama. Guest conductor Leopold Kobin led the Metropolitan Orchestra with Henry Murtagh at the Wurlitzer console.

The final week of Waring's Pennsylvanians saw them co-billed with another Jane and Katherine Lee comedy drama and Theodore Roberts in the film feature *Grumpy*, with May McAvoy and Conrad Nagel. On Saturday, March 17, 1923, Walter Hiers starred in *Mr. Billings Spends His Dime*. Sid's stage show was entitled "A Trip Through the Lasky Studio," with vocalists, ballet, a playlet, and studio models in Harry Fink and Company's 1925 Fashion Show.

Kenneth Taylor in the Los Angeles *Times* of March 18 called the fashion show "a darn good publicity stunt. There were one or two stars and directors the guide forgot to mention yesterday, but that will undoubtedly be attended to immediately. The feminine wearing apparel displayed in the fashion show is enough to set the hearts of the gentler sex a-flutter and possibly remind the money-bearers that the gas is turned off at home or some other excuse to get out. The orchestra under Leopold Kobin plays the overture from 'Mlle. Modiste' and scores again."

The year 1923 was one of Sid's busiest and most productive. Only with staffs who were completely willing to assume enormous burdens of responsibility in management, operation, and maintenance could the shows at the Million Dollar, Rialto, Metropolitan, and Egyptian on Hollywood Boulevard be run as smoothly as they were. One marvels at the inexhaustible vitality that Grauman brought to the managing directorship of these four Los Angeles movie houses.

Sid was probably wise to produce a form of variety stage show at the Metropolitan Theater instead of the theme Prologues that were featured at the Million Dollar Theater, for by presenting dancers, singers, orchestra, and organ specialties in a dazzling vaudeville variety entertainment, he was not competing with the Million Dollar, Rialto, or the Egyptian theaters. Sid was finding an entirely new audience for the big downtown house by presenting fare that closely paralleled the increasingly popular Fanchon and Marco Revues and the Orpheum and Pantages circuits.

In April 1923 the Pennsylvanians were playing at the Million Dollar Theater in a triumphant return to their second Grauman house by popular demand. The Metropolitan Theater was presenting another Paramount feature with Thomas Meighan and Lila Lee, *The Ne'er Do Well*, a Rex Beach story. On the stage was a rare theme show introduced from the Ziegfeld Roof Garden in New York with Ned Wayburn presenting the first of Ben Ali Haggin's tableaux, entitled "Simonetta," and "The Birth of Venus," with Muriel Stryker, Doris Lloyd, Edna French, and a group of glorious American beauties. "Exactly as shown in the Ziegfeld Follies," the ads proclaimed.

The more extravagant Metropolitan shows were often held over, with a slightly altered stage fare, and always with the seventy-piece Metropolitan Orchestra, which was sometimes under the direction of the Great Creatore, who was billed as the world's most eccentric conductor, and later under Herman S. Heller. The large house concentrated on musical presentations that were accompanied by unique lighting effects rather than visual extravaganzas. Sometimes two very different musical aggregations were presented in the same show, such as Ben Black's Syncopating Wizards along with the largest orchestra in the world, as the Metropolitan Symphony was often called. The eminent American composer Charles Wakefield Cadman appeared with the Metropolitan Orchestra to conduct his own compositions during the theater's first year.

On a hot Saturday opening, July 14, 1923, Grauman staged a sparkling ice show on the Metropolitan stage, exactly as it had been presented at the New York Hippodrome. This presentation marked the beginning of theater ice shows on the West Coast and was the precursor of the later Ice Follies. In September, choreographer and dancemaster Theodore Kosloff was featured with artists from the Imperial Russian Ballet in a class performance. By mid-September the ads were calling the Metropolitan stage shows, or at least portions of them, atmospheric Prologues, although they rarely developed thematic material as Grauman did at the Million Dollar and his Hollywood houses.

In October, Sid presented Douglas MacLean in the aerial laugh-riot of the year, *Going Up*. Onstage Sid offered a Prologue called "Aeroplane in Cloudland" with the seventy-piece orchestra under conductor Heller and Murtagh at the Wurlitzer. Whatever the show, and whether portions were held over longer than the usual week's run or went on to other engagements, Grauman stuck to his philosophy of blending shows to contain enough varied elements to appeal to just about everybody. It speaks well for Sid's ability to gauge the public's taste that the new Metropolitan Theater drew consistently large crowds even while the Million Dollar Theater was showing Harold Lloyd's smash hit *Why Worry?*, viewed in its first two record-breaking weeks by twenty-five thousand more patrons than attended in any other two-week period of the theater's history. Even the grand premiere of Mary Pickford starring in Ernst Lubitsch's production of *Rosita* at the Million Dollar Theater, with Mary, Douglas Fairbanks, Charlie Chaplin, and the great Lubitsch himself in person at the opening performance, did not dim the continuing box office success of the largest theater in Los Angeles.

Grauman continued in command of the Metropolitan Theater through July 1924, at which time he sold his interests in the three downtown Los Angeles houses to Famous Players-Lasky (Paramount Pictures). Albert Kaufman became listed as the new managing director of the Million Dollar, and his name also appears as producer of the stage shows at both the Million Dollar and Metropolitan Theater. Grauman concentrated his talents on the long-run policy Egyptian in Hollywood and began to develop plans for the Chinese Theater. The Metropolitan Theater continued to show first-run Paramount pictures and notable variety stage shows, presenting everything from Gilda Gray's sensational shimmy act to a farewell appearance of the female impersonator Julian Eltinge, called "the best dressed woman in the world with his new million dollar gowns never before seen anywhere."

Although the Metropolitan Theater operated as a Publix theater for some years after Grauman relinquished his management, it did not officially change its name to the Paramount Theater until January 24, 1929, with the opening of the all-talking picture, *The Doctor's Secret*, with Ruth Chatterton, H. B. Warner, Robert Edison, and John Loder in the William De Mille production. Accompanying that film were two Publix stage productions, the first a lavish girlie revue from New York, the second a celebration of the New Paramount with George Raft and the Paramount Ballet. Raymond Paige conducted the Paramount Orchestra, Milton Charles played the Wurlitzer, and stars Jean Arthur and Doris Hill officiated as hostesses.

The Paramount Theater continued with stage shows until, like many other large Los Angeles theaters, sound films and the increasing production costs of live shows forced them to devote their programs entirely to films. With many of the great theaters, including the Paramount, now razed and their sites utilized for parking lots or new buildings, it was heartening to read in the June 11, 1979, *New York* magazine that attempts were made to revitalize live shows at the Radio City Music Hall in New York, which had long been famous for two outstanding attractions, its precision-kicking Rockettes and its five-ton, four-thousand-pipe organ, called the world's mightiest Wurlitzer. Besides a $5 million house renovation, all of the leather organ pieces of the Wurlitzer's two hundred thousand moving parts were renewed by hand. A staff organ technician at Radio City Music Hall spent two years on the painstaking task of restoring the huge organ to its original performing perfection and full volume.

The late classical organist Virgil Fox compared playing the Radio City Music Hall Wurlitzer to sitting at the controls of a B-747. His hope was that the Music Hall's management would be persuaded to include a brief organ recital feature in its regular program, and not just use the instrument as background for five thousand people changing seats.

It is also to be hoped that where movie theater organs have remained in their original houses since motion pictures started to talk, these instruments will once again be integrated into regular film performances. One cannot expect to see the recreated splendor of the Grauman Prologues, of course, even though the Radio City Music Hall is featuring the thirty-six Rockettes in twenty-six production numbers and one thousand glittering costumes. But a little live music from the pipe organ could again become the popular theater interlude it once was.

8

On September 26, 1920, the first news story about the construction of what was to be Grauman's Hollywood Egyptian Theater was printed in the real estate section of the Sunday edition of the Los Angeles *Times*. The article stated that

> Sid Grauman plans to build a Class A theater building on Hollywood Boulevard at McCadden Place. The actual property is of unusual shape. The theater auditorium will occupy property on McCadden, but the entrance way will be on Hollywood Boulevard, across the 78-foot frontage where a garden entrance and [rectangular] courtyard will lead to the auditorium [set back] 100 feet from the Hollywood Boulevard sidewalk. A reflecting pool will lie in the center of the courtyard. The theater will be of Spanish style with red tile roofs and archways. The interior motif will also be of Spanish style. The theater will seat 2,000 patrons and have a large balcony. By the deep frontage on McCadden Place, it will allow many exits from the auditorium to accommodate the theater crowds. A full stage will be constructed to allow any type of stage production as well as the presentation of motion pictures. The total cost will be over $500,000.

The publicity story's proposed facts did not all prove out as stated when the theater was completed. For starters, the architecture was changed from Spanish to Egyptian, and the reflecting pool was eliminated as impractical. Also no balcony was ever built, and the orchestra floor accommodated approximately 1,700 patrons, all in stadium-type seating.

The *Times* carried another article on Grauman's Egyptian Theater on October 15, 1922, three days before its auspicious premiere opening. Designed by architects Meyer and Holler, and ultimately finished at a cost of $800,000, the Egyptian's statistics altered dimensionally during its construction. The forecourt became 45 feet wide and 160 feet long, lined on the left side with shops and on the other by a high wall decorated with Egyptian heiroglyphics, glimpsed behind palms and ferns. "The lobby is entered through a colonnade," said the Times, "and the lobby itself is 65 feet wide by 25 feet deep, which leads into a curved foyer. . . . The auditorium is 116 feet wide and 118 feet deep. Seats are arranged on the main floor for 1740 persons divided into a low and a high portion."

An unusual feature of the Egyptian was the location of the organ chamber

beneath the roof above the orchestra pit, which compartment contains a giant Wurlitzer organ. . . . The stage is 30 by 75 feet and is equipped with all of the latest paraphernalia for a speaking stage, flanked by twin columns. An asbestos [fire] curtain spearates stage and auditorium. Ventilation is provided by a system of fans, motors and air washers. Air is drawn through an intake 60 feet high, designed to resemble Cleopatra's Needle. The projection booth

Forecourt of Grauman's Egyptian Theater (1923).

Grauman's Egyptian Theater: proscenium interior with asbestos curtain lowered.

includes two Powers projectors, three spotlights, a Powers triple dissolver, a Westinghouse generator and an Enterprise automatic rewinder for films. The cost of this equipment is reported to have been $5,000. The Theater's electrical work has been arranged in three colors and is controlled from a stage switchboard, connected to a three-dimension system. The auxiliary lighting power is supplied by a battery system. The building is constructed of reinforced concrete with brick filler walls.

This bare description tells very little of the meticulous Egyptian detail with which Grauman decorated the warm dusty pink exterior walls of the theater and the ornate interior. "Grauman built his new showhouse from ideas gleaned from the pages of Egyptian history. Architectural adornment and classical lines that make its construction unique were taken from the time of the ancient builders."

In 1978 the handsome Egyptian Theater became a cluster of three separate theaters, which the

United Artists Theater circuit named Egyptian I, II, and III. The huge columns at the entrance lobby in the rear of the long forecourt were dismantled. A sizable popcorn and candy counter was located to one side of the inner foyer, and the original house was set up as Egyptian I. To reach the small auditoriums of Egyptian II and III, patrons must now walk the length of the forecourt, turn left, and then move through the old exit passageway to a new and separate building located on Las Palmas Place. A small storefront entrance with a ticket office faces west toward the large auditorium wall of the original house.

The October 1922 *Motion Picture News* spoke of Sid's newest theater (which opened before the Metropolitan) as

a cinema temple of great individuality. It is different from anything else in this country [and was much copied]. Furthermore, the policy adopted for this new theater also has individuality. It provides that there shall be but two performances daily, every seat reserved at each performance, and each program to run as long as patronage demands.

The architecture of the new theater is decidedly Egyptian. The entrance . . . is copied from the gateways to Egyptian palaces during the days of Cleopatra, 45 feet wide and 150 feet long. A high garden wall circles to the right. At the base of the wall, a massive fountain sparkles amid tropical verdure. Across the forecourt are numerous foreign shops with stairways which lead to their roofs. From the courtyard, the entrance leads into a lobby under a gigantic colonnade. There are 1,760 seats [varying by 20 from the *Times* report]. A night scene at a ruined temple beside the Nile is painted in oil on an asbestos drop.

The stage has been built to produce any kind of show. The principal support of the roof is an arch with a span of 114 feet. This bears a load of 1,500,000 pounds. Twelve other arches, webbing out over the roof, rest upon the building's principal member. Half of these are in the high roof, the others in the lower portion, all of which are supported on a reinforced concrete truss in front of the proscenium arch.

For the grand premiere of the Egyptian Theater, it was logical that Sid would choose the latest film of one of the world's most popular stars as well as a close friend—the Douglas Fairbanks *Robin Hood*. The press was always effusive about any Grauman opening or new publicity project, but with Grau-

man's Egyptian, the first major house in Hollywood, they outdid themselves. No theater except the later Chinese Theater ever got such exposure in the Los Angeles press.

The *Examiner* talked about the new theater on its opening day, October 18, 1922:

With the opening tonight, Grauman's Hollywood Theater will revive the arts and sciences of long bygone ages, ranging from the infancy of man in the Valley of the Nile to the middle growth through the medieval period in Merrie England and leaping again to its full stature of modern life. This spanning of the centuries will be accomplished through the media of the Egyptian architecture [Howard Carter's discovery of King Tut's tomb had only recently become the international rage] in the new $800,000 film temple. . . .

With a capacity house assured by the advance sale of every seat, a brilliant and glittering assemblage of society leaders and film celebrities will witness the dedication of America's most unique showhouse. . . . The christening ceremonies will begin promptly at 8 o'clock under the personal direction of Sid Grauman, the Southland's master showman. [Director] Fred Niblo will preside during the dedication, in which talks will be given by Mayor George W. Cryer, Jesse

Douglas Fairbanks and Enid Bennett in *Robin Hood* **(1922).**

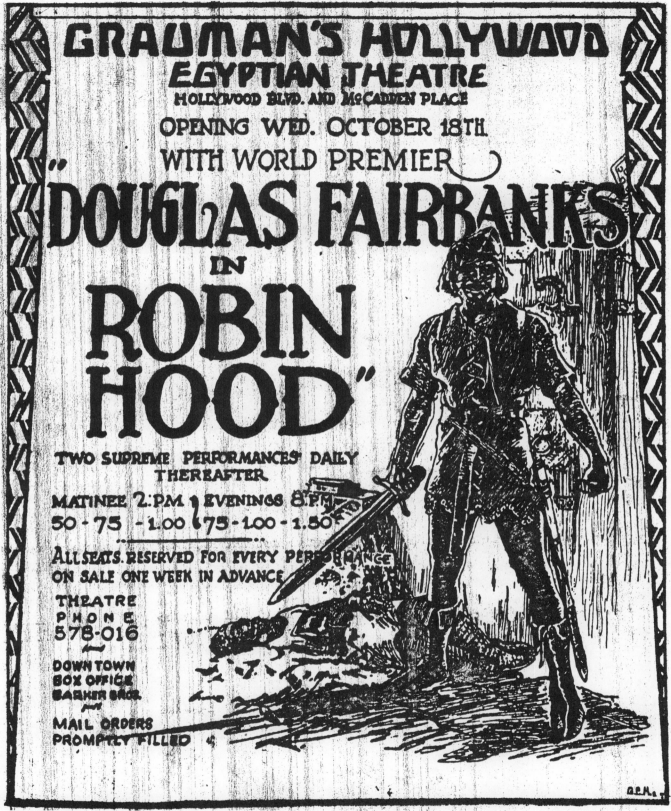

Advertisement for October 18, 1922.

Lasky, Cecil B. De Mille, Charles Chaplin and Hollywood Chamber of Commerce president George L. Bestman. . . . The Nottingham Castle Pageant [using the original film costumes], with music performed by Victor Schertzinger, noted composer and film director, will accompany the film. . . . During its engagement some of the characters who appear in the film will be seen onstage dressed as they were while filming the photoplay. The Pageant [Prologue] will be followed by Robin Hood with Schertzinger conducting the score that he composed for the picture. . . .

The early live portion of the program opened with Verdi's overture to the opera *Aida* with the Egyptian Theater Symphony Orchestra, Jan Sofer conducting. This was followed by an organ recital by Frederick Burr Scholl at the console of the Mighty Wurlitzer, and then the Pageant, one of Grauman's most opulent.

The Egyptian forecourt was brilliantly lighted and the festivities began at 7:00 p.m. in order to give first-nighters ample opportunity to inspect the theater's beauties. One feature that impressed the crowds during the entire time that Grauman managed the Egyptian Theater was the presence of costumed Egyptian sentries walking the parapets, dramatically highlighted against the night. These actors were also there before each matinee performance, calling the faithful to prayer, so to speak. Their highly atmospheric presence added authentic and exotic drama to every performance.

Sid's splendid new Hollywood house with its warm pink and sepia tones and its massive though graceful architecture, was the first photoplay theater in the West to inaugurate the reserved seat policy for all performances. A downtown box office in Barker Brothers at Seventh and Figueroa offered patrons tickets for seats as far as two weeks in advance of the performances. Matinees were given at 2:15 p.m., and evening performances began at 8:15 p.m. The scale of prices for matinees ran from $.50 to $1.00, and evenings from $.75 to $1.50. All performances were offered with full orchestra and Prologue.

Sid's innovative road-show policy made long runs possible; it was no accident that the combination of a dazzling Prologue plus the world premiere of a superior film about a legendary highwayman enjoyed an extensive first-run at the Egyptian Theater which lasted from October 18, 1922, through the first week of April 1923. Grauman proved to

exhibitors everywhere that a first-class film and stage show could make money at legitimate theater prices on a two-a-day performance basis.

A preopening glance at the Prologue for *Robin Hood* led the *Examiner* to praise Grauman's well-known ingenuity, both in the new house and onstage:

> Forty-two centuries may be said to elapse between the setting supplied by the art of the Pharaohs and the imagery that lurks within the brain of Douglas Fairbanks. And over all broods the spell cast first by the Nile by worshippers of Osiris and Isis who have left the record of their loves in hieroglyphics, to live on through the ages to the days of Richard Coeur de Lion, when knighthood flourished throughout the island kingdom. . . . *Robin Hood* breathes the very essence of romance. Over it hovers the witchery of the Crusades, those great religious adventures that made. . .Richard of England an everlasting memory. . . . *Robin Hood in Hollywood* has become Grauman's slogan for the theater's opening, and a blood-and-flesh revue of the famous play's characters within a Nottingham Castle setting onstage is featured during the picture's run. . . . Grauman has engaged the loveliest brunettes he could find in Hollywood to act as usherettes. With their striking beauty, the girls are there in appropriate Egyptian garb to remind patrons of the olden maidens of the Nile.

The core of the Prologue presented a scene at the court of Richard Coeur de Lion, with Maid Marian, the king's jester, Prince John, a knight, Robin Hood, the Cardinal, and five additional knights in attendance. A specialty dancer named Julanne Johnston (later to become a Fairbanks leading lady in *The Thief of Bagdad*) was featured. A group of court ladies, knights of peace, ladies in waiting, flower girls, castle guards, Prince John's men, pages, and servants rounded out the cast of fifty stage actors impersonating their film counterparts in $250,000 worth of magnificent costumes worn in the film production.

Robin Hood, the film, was directed by Allan Dwan from a story by Elton Thomas, and produced by Douglas Fairbanks Pictures Corporation. One of the art directors was young James Mitchell Leisen who was later to become famous as a film director of many successful light comedies in the 1930s. The cast of *Robin Hood* featured Wallace Beery as Richard, Enid Bennett as Lady Marian Fitzwalter; Prince John was Sam de Grasse, Friar

Douglas Fairbanks in *Robin Hood* (1922).

Tuck was Willard Louis, and Little John was Alan Hale, one of the strongest supporting actors Hollywood ever produced. Maine Geary was Will Scarlett, Allan-a-Dale was Lloyd Talman, and, of course, Doug Fairbanks played the Earl of Huntington, afterward Robin Hood.

At midpicture Grauman declared an eight-minute intermission during which the public was invited to stroll in the Egyptian Court and inspect the fine new theater. At the film's conclusion the audience filed out to an original exit march written by Schertzinger and played by the Egyptian Symphony Orchestra.

Although the program sounds rather naive from a 1980s vantage point, accustomed as we are to being bombarded by the dazzling technical advances of stage, screen, and television since 1922,

the Grauman touch packaged cinema entertainment with such skill and loving attention to detail that after opening night the new Egyptian Theater did not need to buy vast advertising space in order to sell the Grauman product. Word of mouth did that so effectively that even after a seven-month run audiences were still drawn to see *Robin Hood*, some patrons having seen the show five or six times.

The redoubtable Douglas Fairbanks also contributed his share to the success of the program with, except for the later *Thief of Bagdad*, perhaps his finest film of all. The *Times*'s Edwin Schallert wrote, "Certainly this is the great picture of the year. That much was established despite the exuberance which attends such a premiere . . .distinguished not only by presentation of a remarkable art work, but by the opening of a beautiful home

Douglas Fairbanks and Wallace Beery in *Robin Hood* (1922).

for pictures right within the precincts of the film capital."

Many people had doubted that a first-class theater such as the Egyptian could draw steady crowds to Hollywood, but after opening night these doubts became supportive praise. Schallert continued: "A new showplace for pictures, a superlatively brilliant premiere, a masterly revelation of cinema technique and feeling—who could ask for more? A night of nights in cinema annals here, making certain a new epoch in the picture art, perhaps even signalizing a new era in the popularizing of the artistic spirit. Everybody from starland was there. Never, perhaps, has there been such an array of gorgeous female attire under one roof. The premiere was a veritable fashion show, in its splendor,

and a garden of beauty as well. Even Charlie Chaplin came to the fore and did that unwanted thing, for him, of saying a few words. He expressed his anticipation of the *Robin Hood* showing, and Charlie did it subtly, for he also indicated that too many speeches palled him. The climax of these preliminaries was the presentation of a laurel wreath to Sid Grauman by Cecil B. De Mille in behalf of the picture folk of Hollywood.

Floral tributes were everywhere, about the entrance court, all betokening the esteem in which Mr. Grauman's accomplishments are held by his many admirers. The theater which Mr. Grauman has built in Hollywood deserves attention, because it is the setting for the place . . . a true theater of the picture type, one in which taste dominates; there is nothing brash about the interior, and naught to distract the eye from the shadowy stage. Lights and decorations all contribute to the spell of reserved splendor. The sphinxes that adorn the proscenium imply that silence is the tribute of appreciation for the visual drama. The Egyptian inscriptions perhaps suggest that mystic incantation of light which gives life to the shadowed surface of the silver sheet. Over all hangs a glorious jewelled sunburst [the central ceiling chandelier] that perhaps heralds the new dawn of the fluent art of the films.

Schallert had quite obviously been hit squarely between the eyes with the atmospheric house and the show itself.

Even today, as one strolls through the Egyptian forecourt to attend a performance at the still-impressive auditorium, it is easy to see why the public of more than fifty-five years ago was duly impressed with the unique house. The architecture was daring for the times and Grauman's staging of the Prologues was often stupendous, always memorable. The music he presented was of top professional quality, and the lighting was the best that most patrons had ever seen on a stage. If Grauman had been lauded previously as a theatrical magician, the opening of the Egyptian Theater and its subsequent string of hit shows continuing through the end of the long-run policy on July 20, 1927, simply reinforced the legend that had started with the Million Dollar Theater.

Sid's shrewd choice of stunning Prologue girls created the most desirable working atmosphere for female entertainers outside of New York, and sometimes led to motion picture and stage stardom. Young women like the beautiful Myrna Loy, singer Benay Venuta, and Latin actress Raquel Torres all began their careers in Grauman Prologues. In 1952 in the Los Angeles *Mirror*, ex-Prologue girl Bee Hunter, then the wardrobe mistress at the Chinese Theater, spoke fondly of her first Grauman job in *The Thief of Bagdad* Prologue to columnist Paul V. Coates.

"I'll never forget the costumes for that show," Hunter reminisced. "Huge, gauzy skirts flecked with real silver. They cost a fortune, all imported material. And bells on our naked ankles. Tiny bras. It was right out of the Arabian Nights. . . . And some of the ideas that Sid used to get! I remember once he sprinkled sugar on the ground near some ants. And then he plotted a whole dance routine from the way the ants marched in and out of that sugar. . . ."

In 1925, the *Examiner* ran a feature on the prototypical chorus girl: PROLOGUE GIRL—DRAMA'S BABY! "Down through the ages from the days of the first chorus has evolved the prologue girl," Leonard Boyd wrote.

Los Angeles is her habitat and she owes her fame to Sid Grauman. . . . More than half a century ago the classicists and romanticists fought a duel to death, resulting in a complete rout of the stilted decorum of the Greek school. Since that time, dramatic evolution has veered toward entertainment of the lighter sort. The first radical change was the introduction of the chorus girl. . . . She came not to edify particularly, but to relieve that fagged out feeling peculiar to most business men. This interloper sang a little, danced a little, winked occasionally and in general was a saucy minx. . . . Soon the box office began to whisper advice. Wise producers began to pick 'em and train 'em. . . . Then came the mannikin girl. . . . And now, thanks to the imagination of men like impresario Sid Grauman, Frank Newman, and the team of Fanchon and Marco, Los Angeles has introduced the world to another distinct species of stage folk, the prologue girl. . . .

She is woven into the fabric of elaborate stage spectacles prefacing feature films. The popularity of such is endorsed by film fans and exhibitors the world over, and the prologue army bids fair to outnumber its fair predecessors. But take it from no less an authority than Sid Grauman, the life of this new species is no bed of roses. . . .

"No after-theater parties or stagedoor johnnies must interfere with her well-ordered routine," Sid advises. "Any attendant caught taking mash notes backstage to the prologue girls will be shot at sunrise. . . . All girls taking part in my present prologue to *The Gold Rush* must follow certain invariable rules. No beauty naps in the morning as rehearsal begins promptly at 8 AM each day. Daily, at an appointed hour, every prologue girl stands to heel for a rigid inspection as to pep, brightness of eye and general health. Twice a week costumes are inspected by the wardrobe mistress who holds each wearer personally responsible. . . . And last but not least, frequent weighing is ordered with recommendations as to food and dieting."

But in spite of this inflexible routine, which Manhattan chorus girls would probably find intolerable, there is little danger, Sid thinks, judging by the throngs seeking a prologue profession, of this newly created species of footlight siren becoming extinct. . . .

On Sunday, January 23, 1923, three days before the opening of the Metropolitan Theater, Sid ran a group ad to cover his downtown theaters and to tout the Egyptian's long-running *Robin Hood*. The Rialto Theater was presenting Adolph Zukor's George Fitzmaurice production of *To Have and to Hold* with Betty Compson, Bert Lytell, Theodore Kosloff, Raymond Hatton, Walter Long, and 2,000 others. Mischa Violin appeared with the orchestra, along with dancers Arnold Tamon and Irene Adams in "The Poetry of Motion." Peter B. Kyne's *The Pride of Palomar* with Marjorie Daw and Forrest Stanley was playing at the Million Dollar Theater along with a Prologue called "A Mid-summer Night in Hobo-land" and featuring a cast of fifty, with Grauman's Symphony Orchestra and Henry Murtagh at the Wurlitzer. A small adjacent ad called attention to Grauman's Sunday Concerts: "Today at 11:30 A.M. 40th Discovery Concert. Henry Murtagh and Genius Discoveries as Soloists. Grauman's Symphony Orchestra, Marcelli conducting. SPECIAL FEATURES: 'Concert Operatic,' Being a Revue of famous operas, interpreted by Orchestra. Instrumental and vocal artists. . . . And then, stay and see *The Pride of Palomar*, and other GRAUMAN features. Reserved seats 35 cents, 55 cents. . . ."

One thing that even Grauman's detractors could not say about him was that he ever shortchanged his customers on quality or quantity. But one incident bears retelling. Sid was an inveterate practical joker; around his town his scapegoats were legion, among them his close friend, Charlie Chaplin. This was one time that Sid became the recipient of a prank.

Being an insomniac, Grauman worked nights, finding that this was the only way to bypass sleeplessness. He often spent nights at his theaters dreaming up new ideas for Prologues into the early morning hours and conferring with his administrative and technical staffs, choosing music, even writing songs, such as his "Au Revoir! Not Goodbye," presented at the Million Dollar Theater.

One night in July 1925, Charlie Chaplin went to the Egyptian box office dressed up as an old grand dame of the mid-Victorian era. The "old lady" appeared to be in high dudgeon and demanded to see the manager personally. When "she" was eventually ushered into Grauman's presence, the showman seated "her" and asked politely what the problem was.

"You're a swindler!" Chaplin shrieked, well into the role of irate female patron. *"The Gold Rush* is a fraud! It's a terrible picture, and what's more, it's immoral. That dance hall girl is little better than a prostitute. You ought to be ashamed of yourself for showing it!"

Grauman's manners were as good as anyone's in Los Angeles show business, but even this was a bit too much for him as the old creature raved on, "And besides, I was deceived by your ad. My seat didn't have a clear view of the stage at all— I couldn't see half the screen."

The old lady rose, brandishing an umbrella. "Young man," Chaplin shrilled, pounding on Grauman's desk, "I *demand* a full refund or I'll take this matter directly to the mayor of Los Angeles!"

Sid's eyes filled with tears—whether genuine or false the story doesn't say—and Chaplin, seeing Sid so morose, broke down, tore off his hat and wig, and began to laugh. Whereupon Grauman drew himself up and said stonily, "Never mind, I'll even things up. Just you wait. . . ."

Sid probably found a way to get back at Chaplin, and apocryphal though the incident may be, it evokes a vivid picture of the kinds of pranks that Grauman and his friends played on one another.

9

THE second long-run feature to play at the Egyptian Theater was Jesse Lasky's production of *The Covered Wagon*. This pioneer epic was directed by James Cruze, its scenario was by Jack Cunningham, and the cameraman was Karl Brown. The saga opened on April 10, 1923, to heavy publicity. Sid Grauman staged another brilliant premiere and packed a distinguished audience into the house for a really superlative bill.

Florence Lawrence reported in the *Examiner* the morning after the opening:

Sid Grauman last night tendered a dedicatory service to Adolph Zukor, Jesse Lasky and James Cruze in honor of their cinematic achievement, *The Covered Wagon*. Stars, directors, technicians paid their fellow workman Cruze the compliment of sincere and obvious appreciation.

The new film is poignant, vital . . . a rhythm of "empire building" . . . that is impelling. Ideals and adventure go hand in hand, romance winds throughout. Death and birth, hardships and rollicking good times vary the sensational river crossings, when spectators thrill with danger . . . at the spirit that animated those early pioneers.

Mr. Grauman offered a prologue of brilliant finesse. He introduced Colonel J. T. McCoy, a United States cavalry officer, who related in detail . . . the dangers . . . in making this picture. [The original program lists Maj. C. Travers as narrator; not so the review. McCoy also appeared later in *The Iron Horse* Prologue bill.] Col. McCoy told of the valiant efforts to achieve realism and authentic historical facts . . . at the end of his speech introducing twenty-five Arapahoe chiefs who participated in the great cinematic spectacle. . . . Following this the Indians offered a campfire scene, a war dance, and a small group of white men made up after the mode of the film carried out much of the action later represented on the silver sheet.

Songs by Charles Wakefield Cadman, "Melodies of a Vanishing Race," were interpolated into the scene . . .

One of the most impressive effects of the Prologue was the clever stage setting, a sheltered valley by a stream. The Indians are watching the arrival on the horizon of a string of covered wagons. Tiny at first in the distance, the wagons as they wind in and out of the rocks grow larger, until they appear onstage finally lifesize, drawn by real horses. The general effect surprised and delighted the audiences at every performance, as did the pageant of Indians, including squaws and papooses, "Forty-niners," pioneers, and more.

The photoplay was adapted from Emerson Hough's novel of the same name. *The Covered Wagon* was one of the first big budget historical films to employ authentic natural settings as a backdrop for its filmed action. Cruze maintained

Sid Grauman with J. Warren Kerrigan and Lois Wilson,
stars of *The Covered Wagon*, at 1923 premiere, in the forecourt of Grauman's Egyptian Theater.

a fine sense of the hardship trek, the imminent
dangers of massacre by the Indians, the starvation
and the low morale. He underscored the tale of
two men in love with the same girl with a delicacy
of touch that occasionally lent the film moments
of rich poetry. Lois Wilson played the girl Milly
for whose affection the rivals, J. Warren Kerrigan
as Will Banion and Alan Hale as Sam Woodhull,
battled it out.

In her review, Lawrence thought Kerrigan "occasionally too good-natured to suit the more rabid
of his spectators, but his revenge is sure, and in the
end his triumph is great." This role marked Kerrigan's return to the screen after a long absence, and
it revitalized his career. Alan Hale added yet another vivid characterization in a subordinate role
to his long list of outstanding film portrayals. Lawrence thought that "perhaps a bit more coquetry

in the opening reels would have added a fillip of
girlish vitality to [Lois Wilson's] part, but in the
end she displays sincere womanliness and admirably poised acting." Lois Wilson's touching performance made her a star.

On December 4, 1923, Grauman brightened
the holiday month with a well-publicized premiere
of Cecil B. De Mille's *The Ten Commandments*.
(This was the first of two versions: silent and in
black-and-white.) Florence Lawrence opened her
review with a biblical quotation:

"And all the people saw the thunderings, the
lightnings and the voice of the trumpet, and
the mountain smoking, and when the people
saw it they trembled." [Or, "removed and stood
far off . . ."] Exodus 20:18.

As the children of Israel first received the ten
commandments when Moses decended from Mt.
Sinai with the stone tablets, so the people of Los
Angeles visioned them last night in the opening
of this tremendous picture at Grauman's Holly-

Indian massacre scene from Jesse Lasky's production of *The Covered Wagon*, directed by James Cruze (1923).

wood Theater . . . . The silver sheet brought visualization of *The Ten Commandments* with impressive grandeur and persuasive beauty. The great foundation laws of the legal writings of most civilized countries of today were presented last night on the screen. Mountains rocked, thunder crashed, flame writ large the commandments on their tablets so that no more laws may be broken through ignorance.

Unquestionably *The Ten Commandments* was considered De Mille's magnum opus up to that time. Both the religious and the scoffers, said Lawrence, must take the film seriously, for it "rings true to drama and religious tenets and offers for the screen a new and mighty evidence of power . . . Theodore Roberts as Moses, Charles de Roche as Pharaoh the Magnificent, Estelle Taylor as Miriam, James Neill as Aaron . . . are excellent." In the modern story's counterpart, Richard Dix, Rod La

Artist Bruce LaLanne's pen-and-ink conception of Sid Grauman's prologue for *The Covered Wagon* at Grauman's Egyptian Theater (1923).

Roque, Leatrice Joy, Nita Naldi, Robert Edeson, and Agnes Ayres played the feature roles. The art direction was by Paul Iribe, and the costumes, both modern and biblical, were designed by Clare West.

The Prologue program was complex. The "Pharoah" Overture was dedicated to Cecil B. DeMille, with Marcelli conducting, and Frederick Burr Scholl on the Mighty Egyptian Symphonic Organ. The second part of the Prologue depicted "The Days of the Glory of the Pharaohs" and presented the principal film characters in the biblical part of *The Ten Commandments*. An Egyptian ballet staged by Fanchon and Marco featured the Dancing Favorites of the Pharaoh. The third part was set at the beginning of Christianity, thirteen hundred years after the Pharaoh, Rameses II. It depicted the Coming of the Messiah [a theme Grauman later explored in the *King of Kings* Prologue], the Three Wise Men, the Nativity of Christ, Christ Healing the Leper, and the Last Supper, a tableau vivant that deeply impressed the audience.

Schallert observed in the *Times,*

Again and again during the long Biblical prologue did the audience of celebrities burst into applause. At times the handclappings were even supplemented by muffled cries and cheers, especially when the full magnitude of such scenes as in the exodus of the children of Israel and the great inundation of the waters of the seas over the heads of Egyptian soldiers was revealed in all its awe-conjuring power. [This same scene was blown up to monstrous proportions in color in the second version.]

One of the finest things [Schallert continued] is the general presentation. Grauman's Egyptian Theater . . . has become renowned for this, and in little more than a year but two different productions have shown there. *The Ten Commandments* is the third, and it might be said that [it] even transcends what audiences recollect as the sovereign appeal of *Robin Hood* and *The Covered Wagon* . . . . The mood is set right at the start, and it must be said without reservation that pictorially it is a highly artistic one. The presentation of Biblical characters is taken right from the film itself. The scene showing the Pharaoh in his great pillared palace is duplicated [onstage] in faithful details, the dancers and figures in the actual drama come to life.

Later we have examples of the art of time carried out in the groupings of the different tableaux. These tableaux, with music, and the songs and dances with which they are blended, comprise both barbaric and highly spiritual motifs, and are away the finest achievements of the kind

that have yet been seen on the stage [Schallert concluded rapturously, having already called the film a super picture], a masterpiece of pictorial impressions whose photographic wonders would remain with audiences for days to come . . .

Seven months later, on July 10, 1924, Sid Grauman premiered the new Douglas Fairbanks film, *The Thief of Bagdad*, the fourth feature to play at the Egyptian Theater under its long-run policy. *Bagdad* played for six months to excellent business. The program opened with a spectacular Prologue titled "The City of Dreams." Set in the marketplace of Bagdad and in the caliph's palace, the Prologue incorporated magicians, dancing girls, eunuchs, and slaves with atmospheric scenes lifted directly from the film. For its time, the artwork and special effects for *Bagdad* were far ahead of other films, and, as usual, the Prologue blended perfectly with the ensuing feature into one intoxicating whole, bizarre and imaginative.

Florence Lawrence said of the *Arabian Nights* film that truly the Orient has moved into Hollywood.

The magic of scenic beauty, the fragrance of roses [wafted through the house], the exotic splendor of stage and film, transformed [the Egyptian] into an Arabian palace last night, which in sheer magnitude of art, astonished the most sophisticated theater-goer. The new Fairbanks film . . . was the motif, and the local premiere attracted an audience which crowded the big auditorium to its doors, and thundered approval of the celluloid masterpiece of fantasy and optical charm.

To the brilliance of the film, Sid added a masterly prologue [Lawrence said]. Here in dramatic and rhythmic gestures was told the tale of an Arabian wedding. Princes, slaves and caliphs marched straight out of the film apparently, and gave in living, breathing reality a brief portion of the fabulous love story of the silver sheet. Dancers, conjurors, nautch maidens, voices from the mosque, and all that helps to weave the spell of magic and mysticism, were vivid features. . . . The audience breathed the very essence of Araby in the beauty and radiance of the evening.

The overture "City of Dreams" was played by the symphony orchestra with guest conductor Mortimer Wilson wielding the baton in Oriental costume. Immediately following the overture, John Steele was cordially greeted by the large audience and presented various members of the cast who walked to the orchestra pit, where in a blaze of spotlights, the audience was saluted. . . .

Grauman's Egyptian Theater in Hollywood during run of
Douglas Fairbanks's *The Thief of Bagdad* (1924).

On July 11, the morning after the opening, Schallert of the *Times* called the premiere dazzling. "*The Thief of Bagdad* is playing at last, and it is a banquet royal of film entertainment. The premiere may have been . . . the most brilliant; though summer is not the time for the most resplendent social audiences, certainly this presentation lured forth a glamorous representation. . . . Never has there been so much . . . carnival . . . and so much of light and gaiety, not only of the playhouse itself but virtually all the Boulevard in the immediate vicinity."

The crowds stretched for blocks, and the approach to the Egyptian forecourt had to be kept open by special police.

"The Egyptian," Schallert went on,

has become the center for the great premiers in this locality . . . the home of features destined for long runs. Only three films have been displayed there in nearly two years, and *Robin Hood*, Doug's previous spectacle . . . opened the theater . . . . Doug was absent from the occasion [*Bagdad*] . . . he was travelling in France. While

the prologue may never be as immensely commended as the one for *The Ten Commandments*, it is evidence of Sid Grauman's tremendous showmanship. He has caught the real spirit of the fantasy. There is one of the most gorgeous displays of costumes that has ever been seen on the stage. . . . Some of the dances, especially those that are eccentric in character, conjure up not only the mood of the production, but call forth a lot of humor from the audience besides. . . . The craftsmanship of this stage spectacle is magnificent. . . . I have seen [dances] created by Ruth St. Denis and Pavlova that were no more of popular interest. It is an achievement indeed that Mr. Grauman has been able to go so far in perfecting an ensemble of terpsichoreans and a pageant to achieve such a lovely, colorful and artistic result . . . . He has carried out the same result in the exterior decorations of the esplanade, which last night was filled in every nook and corner with people waiting to glimpse the stars. Incense burned everywhere, multicolored balloons hovered overhead, various figures of oriental dieties are glimpsed here and there. Really, *The Thief of Bagdad* has changed the whole atmosphere of this section of Hollywood into a sort of Arabian Nights fantasy in itself . . . . The ushers wear long harem veils and their dancing girl costumes mingle colors of exotic softness. The orchestra and conductor ap-

91

pear in turbans and sheik costumes. The stage is transformed right from the beginning into a picture of bazaars, hanging rugs, carved archways and minarets, everything symbolical of the Orient. By degrees this vista of beauty gives way to the all-important culminating event, the screening of *The Thief of Bagdad* . . . .

On December 6, 1924, Grauman opened his next Egyptian program with Lillian and Dorothy Gish in *Romola*, preceded by an auspicious Prologue. Lillian Gish was one of the finest serious actresses of the early screen and is today perhaps the most unsung among the founding Hollywood stars for her acting achievements with D. W. Griffith, and afterwards. Sister Dorothy was an adroit comedienne of great charm, although she did not have the dramatic depth of Lillian. The latter was at her most heartbreaking as Hester in the silent version of *The Scarlet Letter,* in which she co-starred with Lars Hanson. She also adapted the Hawthorne novel with scenarist Frances Marion.

The Gish sisters lived in New York, and often worked on Broadway. For *Romola* they were persuaded to journey west for one of their rare premiere appearances where they were loudly cheered by adoring fans.

Schallert called the premiere "an event emblazoned in the film theatrical history of Los Angeles. And as usual," he hastened to add, "Sid Grauman has provided a tremendously effective prologue, the outstanding episode . . . a carnival scene . . . from . . . the picture. He has made a real carnival with dancers and pageantry, and a troupe of acrobats that veritably stop the show. The presentation is a true treat to the eye in its life and picturesqueness, admirably staged.

"After the picture, Lillian and Dorothy were introduced to the audience, and almost overwhelmed with applause. By smiles and words . . . they indicated their delight at being present for the glamorous reception. . . ."

The *Times* featured a photograph of the Gish sisters on its front page, showing Dorothy, Lillian, and their mother disembarking from the Los Angeles-bound train at the Santa Fe depot. *Romola* was set in Renaissance Italy, with Ronald Colman as the hero and a newcomer, William Powell, as the villain. Filmed entirely on location in Florence, Italy, the film was Lillian's second European venture, the first being *The White Sister*, also with Colman. *Romola* was released by Metro-Goldwyn-

Dorothy Gish and Kid McCoy in *Memories*, **Majestic Studios, Yonkers, New York.**

Mayer and shown on December 1, 1924, at the George M. Cohan Theater in New York. Lillian Gish recalls that it opened five days later at the Chinese Theater in Hollywood. Her date is right, but she had the wrong theater. The Chinese had not yet been built.

Romola was a good story and a fair picture, but it did not enjoy the long run that other features had at the Egyptian. The premiere, however, was a brilliant one and the film was well attended.

During their visit to Los Angeles, the Gish sisters stayed at the Ambassador Hotel where Sid Grauman resided in a suite with his mother, Rosa. Mary Pickford came to call on the Gish ladies, who were back in Los Angeles after a six-year absence. The fetes planned for the sisters had to be cancelled because the day after their premiere appearance for Grauman they were forced by a business commitment to climb aboard the eastbound California Limited and head back to New York.

A day before the opening of the next feature at the Egyptian Theater, *The Iron Horse*, a publicity stunt was staged in Hollywood on February 20, 1925. "A steel monster from the days of 1863," the news release said,

but a quaint old brass-bound locomotive today, the Collis P. Huntington, historical engine of the Central Pacific, was acclaimed all along the line yesterday as it was towed through Hollywood in a parade [to advertise *The Iron Horse* premiere].

The patriarch of the rails hauled the first transcontinental train in 1869 when East and West were united by rail. The locomotive was brought to Hollywood by Sid Grauman in connection with the presentation of *The Iron Horse*, John Ford's screen drama of the winning of the West, its premiere at The Egyptian tonight. Grauman, railroad officials, cast members of the film, Arapahoe and Shoshone Indians who appear in the prologue to the screen drama rode the engine in the parade with cowboys from the Fox studio as escorts. . . .

The Iron Horse opened at the Egyptian on February 21, 1925. It was Ford's most important picture to date, produced and directed by the young filmmaker for William Fox. Sid Grauman's Prologue for the film was called "The Days of 1863--1869" and its scene was Promontory, Utah, at the time of the building of the transcontinental railroad. The overture was a medley of old-time favorites, with airs "your grandparents used to sing" played by Grauman's Egyptian Orchestra, Marcelli conducting, and Frederick Burr Scholl at the Mighty Egyptian Organ.

The eight-part Prologue introduced Colonel T. J. McCoy in person. The program refers to McCoy as "a great American authority on the vanishing race. McCoy has lived most of his life with the Indians on the reservations." The colonel then presented

At the premiere of *The Iron Horse*, **Grauman's Egyptian Theater, 1925.** *Left to right*: **Mrs. Grauman, Judge Charles Edward Bull (who played Abe Lincoln), Sid Grauman, and Mrs. Bull.**

twenty-five Shoshone and Arapahoe Indians with their squaws and papooses. "The finest types of Redmen to be found in America today." Next came Chief Yawlache, singing native melodies, followed by "Tabloids of the Pioneer Days," accompanied by colorful lighting effects, presenting "the real American Indians and Plainsmen." Next was a "Selected Novelty" and then the "Days of 1863–1869 at Promontory, Utah: The loyal track layers laying the rails of the first transcontinental railroad nearing its destination." This was climaxed by the arrival onstage of two locomotives, there for the driving of the final spike to connect the two great railroads. The celebration of this important event was ritualized by the Hoop Skirt Dance arranged by Fanchon.

The Iron Horse starred George O'Brien as Davy Brandon, with Fred Kohler, J. Farrell MacDonald, Madge Bellamy, and quite literally a cast of thousands—a regiment of United States troops and cavalry; 3,000 railway workmen; 1,000 Chinese laborers; 800 Pawnee, Sioux, and Cheyenne Indians; 2,800 horses; 1,300 buffalo; and 10,000 Texas steers. A program note explained that the actual old-time locomotives and equipment that figured in the building of the transcontinental railway were used throughout *The Iron Horse.* They were "Jupiter" of the old Central Pacific, and the "116" of the Union Pacific.

Andrew Sinclair, in his recent biography of John Ford, points out that *The Iron Horse* was meant to be William Fox's epic answer to *The Covered Wagon.* "Ford was the right director for the job," says Sinclair. He set up a camp in the Nevada Desert to bunk and feed the four thousand extras who played the Irish and Chinese railroad builders.

If the plot of *The Iron Horse* is melodramatic, with its hero George O'Brien somewhat vapid and exaggerated, Ford achieved a final grandeur with the driving of the last spike in the link between the Atlantic and Pacific coasts, and the meeting of the two locomotives to open the track, and the concluding shot of Abraham Lincoln with the caption, "His truth is marching on."

In one particular back-tracking shot where a railroad man on a handcar sees his brother falling to his death from a telegraph pole, Ford showed his genius in his portrayal of the insignificance of one human life measured against the large historical view. Somewhere between the heroic myth of the past and our common hu-

George O'Brien in the role of Davy Brandon, pony express rider, in the John Ford production of *The Iron Horse*, a William Fox presentation.

manity lay Ford's own vision, most true when it contrasted both the effort and pettiness of men's work against the scale of nature.

Ford's epic cost $280,000 to make, and grossed more than $3 million, a spectacular sum for the time. Ford refused to attend the opening night, hating the publicity. *The Iron Horse* was the only large-scale epic that John Ford ever made.

With a musical score especially created for the film by Erno Rapee, the epochal silent feature captured immediate popularity and played to packed audiences long after it departed the Egyptian Theater to make way for Charlie Chaplin's *The Gold Rush*, which arrived on June 26, 1925.

The day *The Gold Rush* opened at the Egyptian there were reams of publicity in the local newspapers, for a Grauman opening had now become an event that attracted celebrities and the general public alike. Anyone who could secure a ticket was lucky, and those who could not massed themselves outside the theater along Hollywood Boulevard to cheer the arriving patrons.

The premiere was also the debut of Charlie

The Gold Rush, with Charlie Chaplin, premiered with a prologue at Grauman's Egyptian Theater in 1925.

Chaplin's fourth feature-length comedy drama. The *Times* publicity release promised that "almost every picture star, producer, and studio executive have made reservations for parties."

Celebrities began to arrive at the theater by 8:30 p.m. and were promptly introduced by "a new system of announcing personages" over loudspeakers. Grauman asked that the regular first-nighters and the society patrons please be in their seats by no later than 8:20 p.m. so that the entrance of the stars would not be delayed. "The exhibitor of prologue fame has spared no pains or expense in preparing a scintillating spectacle. Alaska in the days of the Klondike Gold Rush will be presented in an elaborate ten-act prologue to introduce the master comedian's most pretentious production. Those who have had a peep at Grauman's spectacle pronounce it an epoch-making exhibition. . . . A musical score has been arranged for *The Gold Rush* by Carli D. Elinor, a composer famed for such adaptations. The premiere will introduce to the public the Egyptian Orchestra leader, Gino Severi, and Julius K. Johnson at the console of the great Egyptian organ. . . ."

Schallert of the *Times* was as impressed with the premiere as a spectacle as he was with *The Gold Rush.*

Charlie sets a pace for length in the lighter sort of entertainment, and though it is not all gay in any manner of means, its premier appeal is for merriment. The [world premiere] was held last night at The Egyptian, noted for its many bril-liant openings in the past several years. [This] surpassed by far all the others.

Chaplin's productions are not a matter of monthly or even yearly routine in the theater. . . His position as leader of the industry, the fact that his new comedy has been termed revolutionary . . . and the interest that has been directed toward him through his marriage [to Lita Grey] and various other circumstances, all contributed to intensify to white heat the interest in *The Gold Rush.*

At no more auspicious a time could the opening have been held. [Charlie's first marriage to adolescent Lita and the early birth of their first child was juicy gossip for Hollywood and the world.] The West has seldom been host to such a huge assemblage of more prominent stars. Douglas Fairbanks and Mary Pickford have seldom been among the big premiere audiences here [not even for their own pictures], nor have Lillian Gish [back in town after a stay in New York], John Barrymore and others who graced the theater last night. . . . In the comedian's work there is not, I feel, quite so much of his wonted spontaneity. There are many delicious moments but there are others more than inclined to be a trifle forced. . . . In any event, the picture is one that commands a certain high admiration for its daring, and there is no lack of interest and entertainment while it is going on. The final sequence . . . discloses Chaplin in fashionable clothes and enables him to afford a new and very interesting highlight on his work. . . .

Schallert made no mention of the Prologue called "Charlie Chaplin's Dream" in his review, although it was carefully planned and one of Grauman's best. The Prologue opened with a tribute to *The Gold Rush* by prominent stars of the industry in a short film made especially for the premiere performance. After the traditional overture and an organ interlude came "The Land of the Midnight Sun," a fantasy about a lonely prospector who meets Eskimos, dances with them, and joins in their fun, ending with Charlie's dream. First came the moods of the Northland in "The Spirit of the Frozen North," and afterwards a "Balloon Dance" by Lillian Powell, then a festival of ice skaters brilliantly costumed, and a scene in the Monte Carlo dance hall in the Yukon, followed by Charlie's awakening.

Sid Grauman had special associations with the subject of the Chaplin film, drawing on his own Dawson days for much of the Prologue's atmosphere. Having lived in the Yukon, Sid knew exactly what the Monte Carlo dance hall should look like on the stage, and the audience was enchanted with its gaudy realism that added another successful theme show to the long list that Grauman had already produced. *The Gold Rush* played at the Egyptian Theater for a little over four months, companioned by Grauman's unique Prologue with 100 people on the stage, as distinct a hit in its own right as Chaplin's innovative feature.

In all of Grauman's theater programs he gave credit where possible to his Prologue assistants and to the studio staffs of the movies he exhibited. It has been said of Sid that he dominated the publicity releases from his theaters to an unwarranted degree. But if this is true, then one must ask the question: What would the shows have been without Sid's perceptive, guiding brilliance and originality? And he did acknowledge support. Today's film credits are usually rolled almost as fast as television credits, and names are often lost in the rush. This was not the case in Grauman theater programs.

The next feature to play the Egyptian Theater was King Vidor's production of *The Big Parade*, the first great film about World War I, which starred John Gilbert, with Renee Adoree, Karl Dane, Tom O'Brien, Hobart Bosworth, and Claire MacDowell in featured roles. The film opened on November 2, 1925, and played for almost six months. A small boxed note in the original program proclaims, presumably to discourage false advertising, "Grauman's Egyptian Theater, Hollywood, is the only institution of its kind in the world, and is the only theater with which Sid Grauman has any connection, Mr. Grauman having disposed of his entire holdings in any other playhouses, in which he was formerly interested several years ago."

In a column by Jack Smith of the *Times* on March 19, 1978, some fifty-three years later, the Los Angeles writer discussed with King Vidor the nostalgic data on the making of *The Big Parade*, which cost $240,000 to film and was a sensational success at the Egyptian. "I made it for only $200,-000," Vidor told Smith, "but Irving Thalberg wanted a night battle scene, and that cost $40,000 more. It ran . . . two years at the Astor in New York and made $22 million. It put Metro-Goldwyn-Mayer on the map and was the *Star Wars* of its time. . ."

Vidor explained to Smith that not a single foot of film was shot in France. The French village was

Scene from King Vidor's production of *The Big Parade*, starring John Gilbert, Renee Adoree, and Karl Dane (MGM 1924).

built on the Metro-Goldwyn-Mayer back lot, and the battle scene was filmed in Elysian Park. "Our Belleau Wood," said Vidor. "I got many letters from marines and soldiers saying it looked exactly like Belleau Wood. I was in my 20s still and had never been to Europe. When I went to Belleau Wood, I thought Elysian Park looked better . . . Andrew Wyeth wrote me that the scene [the last in the picture, in which John Gilbert minus a leg comes back to France to claim Renee Adoree in the fields ploughing] had influenced him more than any other. I took the print back and we saw it together. He said he had copied the hill in his paintings. . . ."

Along with *The Big Parade*, Grauman presented his "Memories of 1918" Prologue set in two scenes. The first was "Somewhere in France" and revealed doughboys at rest near the front, with Red Cross nurses and the entertainers who brought some enjoyment to the soldiers' lives. The second scene was an Armistice Day pageant, with dances, tableaux, and the presentation of the Allies' colors: Italy, Belgium, France, Scotland, England, and the United States.

Sid's Prologue was one of the most elaborate he had ever attempted, which says a lot, considering the lavish spectacles he had staged since the opening of the Million Dollar Theater. The *Times* said that "Grauman clothed the stage in beauty and symbolic power, and the tableaux and ballets augmented the patriotic note which the picture also exalts. . . . But despite the glamour of the prologue, it was in the picture itself that the audience found its greatest thrill. Heralded in advance as one of the finest pictures ever made the new film met

with storms of applause, gales of laughter, excitement and torrential emotional waves which testified to its success."

King Vidor went on to make many other fine films, whereas Gilbert was unsuccessful in adapting his talents to the spoken film medium. It was not Gilbert's voice that failed him, as some claimed; it was his ineptitude with the awful dialogue of those early sound pictures.

On November 6 the *Examiner* ran a piece about the Los Angeles veterans' organization and the regular army troops marching down Hollywood Boulevard to herald the opening of *The Big Parade*. Thirty motorcycle officers formed a vanguard, and leading the parade was Grand Marshal Major L. Chambers from Fort MacArthur. Among the various military ensembles participating was Sid Grauman's Black Falcons, an organization of reserve aviators, sponsored by Sid, which surely must have helped to implement the publicity stunt. There was

Renee Adoree and John Gilbert in *The Big Parade*.

Trench scene from *The Big Parade* **with Karl Dane, John Gilbert, and Tom O'Brien.**

a *Big Parade* float, a reproduction of a trench machine gun emplacement manned by six doughboys in khakis. Red fire along the line of march lent a carnival effect, the article said.

Two months later a large advertisement ran in the Examiner: "STARS WILL MANAGE THE EGYPTIAN THEATER THIS EVENING. JOHN GILBERT will sell seats in the box office—RENEE ADOREE will be distributing programs—KARL DANE and TOM O'BRIEN will usher—KING VIDOR will take tickets for THE BIG PARADE. Can you imagine the thrill of visiting a theater with this galaxy of M–G–M celebrities attending you? It is an event that happens once in a lifetime. . . . And Remember . . . SID GRAUMAN'S PROLOGUE with 150 people On the Stage will never be seen elsewhere. . . ."

Sid did not pass up the smallest opportunity to promote the Egyptian Theater. The Hollywood Boulevard house in its prime under Grauman was without doubt the best-known film theater in America, drawing locals and tourists to its long-run, two-a-day performances by the hundreds of thousands.

In 1969 the Egyptian Theater was completely renovated by United Artists in a six-week, full-time $250,000 remodeling project. The first Dimension 150 screen in Hollywood was installed. It was seventy-five feet wide, and to accommodate it the old proscenium was enlarged to a width of eighty feet. Pillars and sphinx heads were removed, and the screen was set back twenty-seven feet to the rear stage wall. The projection booth, at mezzanine level during Grauman's tenure, was relocated on the main floor reducing the seat count from 1,770 to 1,340.

10

IN the *Examiner* of May 2, 1926, there was planted a publicity item about the Egyptian's forthcoming double bill starring the king and queen of Hollywood, Doug Fairbanks and Mary Pickford. "GRAUMAN BUSY ON DUAL PREMIER PLANS," the story stated. "Something new in show business on Friday Evening, May 14th. Sid Grauman has booked two feature motion pictures into his Hollywood Egyptian Theater that are playing separately in New York at $2.00 admission price [each]. The new program will star Mary Pickford and Douglas Fairbanks in their films *The Black Pirate* and *Sparrows*. On stage will be two preludes to the feature attractions. Grauman is busy rehearsing the two prelude casts. This is a new idea in entertainment presentations," the item claimed, and it surely was, being the original first-run double bill.

Doug and Mary were in Europe and not available for personal appearances at the premiere, but this didn't stop Sid from exploiting the situation. On May 13, a publicity release appeared in the *Times*:

The trans-Atlantic cables will carry the longest report of a theatrical event ever to be transmitted under the sea after midnight tomorrow, addressed to Mary Pickford and Douglas Fairbanks in Europe and giving all the details of Sid Grauman's duplex premiere of their latest feature productions . . . . In a recent cable, Mary and Doug who are en route from Italy to Berlin, instructed their representatives here to file a complete story on the . . . famous stars of filmland who will attend the function, the novel stunts Sid Grauman has planned to feature the opening, and a description of the spectacular preludes of the two productions. The trans-ocean wires with which he will usher in the first presentation of the two productions. The trans-ocean wires will carry a voluminous report of the reception and notables, as presented by Fred Niblo, master of ceremonies, as well as expressed views on the presentations, the pictures and the accompanying musical scores, which Grauman has had specially written for the premiere.

While Mary's *Sparrows* was filmed in black and white, Doug's swashbuckling *The Black Pirate* was "a triumph in Technicolor." An advertisement in the *Times* of May 13 said that "the most brilliant audience the world has ever known will . . . attend this first duplex premier featuring the two most beloved stars of the screen, each in their own productions preceded by novel Sid Grauman preludes. In no other theater in the world will these two masterpieces be seen together. The magnitude of the program [with reserved seats going at $5.00 for opening night] demands that everyone be seated by 8:10 p.m."

Mary Pickford on the set of *Sparrows*. Film premiered at Grauman's Egyptian Theater on a double bill with a Douglas Fairbanks production of *The Black Pirate*.

Needless to say, with the combined attractions of two films and two preludes, even the press was suitably inclined to praise. Schallert said that Mary Pickford conquered over Doug, accomplishing her greatest cinematic triumph.

A threefold contest was won Friday night at the Egyptian . . . that will be historically remembered not only for weeks and months, but as a famous song writer [Irving Berlin] would have it, perhaps even for "always" in the annals of film. . . . The combination of the two productions with the incidental prologue and preludes---that's a new one---that Grauman has provided is easily the most elaborate and highly contrasted presentation, I would like to say banquet, only it does not fit the occasion, that has without question been contrived . . . . Fred Niblo said that Doug liked to have his pictures presented at the theater so much that this time he brought Mary along with him. With such a neatly worded preamble . . . the wavering doubts that many had felt regarding the Grauman presentation were all but removed. And it took only the weeping power and pathos of Mary's most beautiful and telling of story interpretations to carry victory to its completeness. . . . Fortunately, the abundance of program . . .

proved an exceedingly well-balanced affair. The two films are each in an entirely different mood. Mary's is heavy and dramatic, but absolutely masterful in the way it reaches its audience. The other is pictorially resplendent with a wealth of color photography made manifest in its finer values for probably the first time. . . .

Schallert much preferred Mary's *Sparrows*, although he still conceded Doug the crown for adventure. "Whether *The Black Pirate* will ever start a rage for color photography, used throughout the film, may be doubted, but it is nevertheless a great advancement along new lines of beauty. . . . Sid proffers an intimate novelty in his depiction of the arrival of stars at the Grauman Theater. The audience enjoyed especially the songs of 'Hollywood's Most Picturesque Character' whom you know in advance is the singer these numbers portray. All you need to do is to take a glance up at the new widely recognized gentleman in sheik's garb who marches back and forth on the high promenade as you enter the theater. . . ."

The double bill played into mid-August and finally gave way to the premiere on August 20, 1926, of the Warner Brothers production of *Don Juan*, starring John Barrymore and Mary Castor with a huge cast. That summer was beginning to prove what Grauman had always known about Hollywood—it was not only the film capital of the world, it was becoming a leading center of theater entertainment as well. The *Examiner* declared that the combined seating capacity of Hollywood's theaters would soon be able to accommodate 21,000 patrons. "Many new showhouses are under construction and planned for Hollywood. The new El Capitan Theater [legitimate] opened recently, and Warner Brothers and Sid Grauman have plans to construct new theaters on Hollywood Boulevard. Publix Theaters Corporation will build a new 4,000-seat theater at Vine and Sunset. Wilkes' Vine Street Theater is now being constructed on Vine south of Hollywood Boulevard. Another legitimate theater, the Music Box, is underway on the Boulevard, east of Vine, and will be the home of musical revues." (The international hit, *Charlot's Revue*, starring Gertrude Lawrence, Jack Buchanan, and Beatrice Lillie opened at El Capitan on May 3, 1926, to an enthusiastic press.)

The following month a newspaper headline stated that Sid Grauman reputedly had the contract for Cecil B. De Mille's *King of Kings* to open his new Chinese Theater sometime in 1927.

At the Egyptian, *Don Juan* proved to be a dark and somber affair, and although faithful to the legend, it was not a great popular success, even with the charismatic John Barrymore in the title role. An elaborate electrical display with a titanic rainbow as its crowning feature projected skyward from the Egyptian's roof by searchlights and fascinated the crowds. Hollywood Boulevard was illuminated in front of the theater as if it were midday.

with ensembles of singers and dancers. Grauman dispensed with the regular theater curtain in favor of a huge Venetian blind. In the movie cast with Barrymore and Astor were Estelle Taylor, Jane Winton, Montague Love, Warner Oland, Phyllis Haver, and Hedda Hopper (later to be Louella O. Parsons's rival).

What attracted the public even more to the presentation of *Don Juan* during its run was a screen that made recognizable musical sounds for the first time in its short history. Vitaphone, through the auspices of Warner Brothers, had finally made it to the big time, and although nobody thought so then, sound would soon be around films for good and would completely dominate motion pictures.

On October 5, ads began to appear announcing the arrival of Vitaphone at Grauman's Egyptian Theater. This event would be solemnized by a grand premiere to be held on October 27, in conjunction with the current showing of *Don Juan*. Patrons at the Egyptian could then hear the New York Philharmonic Orchestra of 107 pieces with soprano Anna Case, violinist Efrem Zimbalist, pianist Harold Bauer, and violinist Mischa Elman—all for the price of the regular admission, "*seen* and *heard* simultaneously ON THE SCREEN," the ads underscored. "You actually feel the magnetism of their [the artists'] personality. Vitaphone is made possible through years of experimentation and co-operation by four great companies: Warner Brothers, Vitaphone Corporation, Western Electric and the Bell Telephone Laboratories."

Although musical accompaniment to films by large orchestras was not exactly unknown to Grauman audiences, sound emanating from the screen was a distinct and exciting novelty. Sid made the most out of this stunning innovation by presenting world-famous artists in what amounted to little more than vaudeville turns. The stage-trained John Barrymore was not yet speaking on film, however. That would come later when he made an auspicious talking picture debut in the 1929 screen revue, *The Show of Shows*, playing a scene from *Richard III*.

With the assist of the Vitaphone featurettes, *Don Juan* lasted another three weeks at the Egyptian. It was followed by Syd Chaplin playing Old Bill in *The Better Ole* on November 17, 1926, plus Vitaphone shorts.

The Better Ole was given a sparkling premiere, as befitted the extremely talented and often overshadowed brother of Charlie. Sharing the film's reception was Syd Chaplin in person, who was introduced warmly by Sid Grauman. Through the wonder of Vitaphone some of stageland's greatest favorites were presented: Al Jolson, Georgie Jessel, Elsie Janis, Willie and Eugene Howard, and opera baritone Reinald Werrenrath. The arrival of stars, directors, producers, and society leaders was broadcast in detail over radio station KFWB, the Warner Brothers outlet, to the home-sitting public and through loudspeakers to the ecstatic throngs that crowded Hollywood Boulevard outside the theater.

Syd Chaplin's film concerned an irrepressible British Tommy and was drawn from the stage play based on Bruce Bairnsfather's cartoon character. Grauman introduced the picture to his premiere audience with a special synchronized Vitaphone background. Schallert said in the *Times* that there was "strong evidence of interest in both phases of the program, and a response of laughter for the Chaplin film that he quite merited this recognition. . . . The Vitaphone program aims very largely at a lighter popular appeal on this occasion, with the exception of a couple of bromidic solos by Reinald Werrenrath, 'Long, Long Trail' and 'When You Look in The Heart of A Rose' . . . Shades of antiquity!" Schallert, however, found the Jolson Vitaphone turn lifelike.

There were moments when the illusion of his presence was very nearly perfect. . . . There are things yet to be accomplished in the registering of voices in talk, especially on the Vitaphone, and some sort of measuring devised to determine just how long an audience will laugh over a certain joke. Several times smart lines were lost because the echoes of mirth had not died down in the house when Jessel resumed talking. . . . The reproduction of sound was not quite as good, I felt, as at the showing given with *Don Juan*. . . . The musical accompaniment to *The Better Ole* WAS inclined at times to be heavy . . . and the musical scoring of comedy pictures especially will have to be done with a deft hand in the future. . . . "Tipperary" was sung during the marching, and there were some incidental shoutings during the show, given by soldiers. . . .

As if responding to the trend of things to come by intuition, Sid had discontinued his famous Prologues with the showing of *Don Juan* and *The Better Ole* in order to introduce Vitaphone sound and pictures to the public in late 1926. This abrupt and dramatic elimination of the Prologue, a Grauman hallmark, caused disappointment among audiences and near hysteria among singers, dancers, actors, and instrumentalists who were regularly employed in the Grauman spectaculars. The Vitaphone system also caused repercussions in other areas of entertainment, although at the time no one, not even the prescient Sid, could foresee the extent to which the talking screen would alter the techniques and social structure of the entire motion picture industry and the entertainment world in general.

The year 1927 arrived with Grauman still featuring the Vitaphone acts, now billed over Syd Chaplin's *The Better Ole*. This bill bowed out in late January to make way for Adolph Zukor's and Jesse Lasky's production of James Cruze's *Old Ironsides*. It is easy to imagine that Grauman was far more concerned with the details of progress of the rising Chinese Theater, then nearing its completion, than with the novelty of Vitaphone at the Egyptian. Sound was advanced enough then to become an instant threat to silent pictures and the jobs of Prologue people. The complaints Sid must have received about his discontinuance of the Prologues from public and press alike may have forced him to reinstate the theme shows with *Old Ironsides*, which opened at the Egyptian on January 28, 1927, with a Prologue.

Old Ironsides was the sentimental story of the U.S.S. *Constitution*, the forty-four-gun frigate that was perhaps the most famous vessel in U.S. naval history. Launched in 1798, she participated in the Tripolitan War, the War of 1812. She was rebuilt in 1833, laid up at the Portsmouth navy yard in 1855, and used as a training ship. Rebuilt again in 1877, the *Constitution* crossed the Atlantic, and in 1897 she was stored at the Boston navy yard. By popular subscription in 1925, she was rebuilt once more. As the movie *Old Ironsides* was released, the venerable ship was undergoing reconstruction.

The film drew the same sort of crowds that other spectacles such as *The Iron Horse* and *The Covered Wagon* had attracted to the Egyptian Theater. Back in good form was the Grauman Prologue, this time the colorful "100 Years Ago." An "Old Ironsides" overture was conducted by Constantin Bakaleinikoff, with Edgar Eugene Eben at the Mighty Egyptian organ. The Prologue opened at Independence Hall, Philadelphia, October 22, 1797. A celebration was in progress the night before the launching of the *Constitution*. President John Quincy Adams made a facsimile appearance, and John Maxwell, the singing sensation of the century, entertained—although the program does not make clear whether Maxwell was the name of a contemporary artist or a historical figure. The scene then shifted to George Washington's Home with the Tiny Tots Ballet. (How Grauman made such a switch must be chalked up to his uncanny ability to mix visual non sequiturs and make audiences accept them without question.) Next came the arrival of the immigrants, introducing the Koshetz Ukrainian Singers, followed by a Ballet of the Ship. "Colored servants" performed as emperors of harmony, and the Prologue closed with a final tabloid, "The Birth of the American Flag" with assorted guests, naval officers, and citizens of Philadelphia. Staged by Sid with loving care, the Prologue was choreographed by Ernest Belcher, the popular ballet master.

Old Ironsides starred blonde Esther Ralston and Charles Farrell as the lovers, Wallace Beery as the boatswain, and George Bancroft as the gunner. The famous world-champion Hawaiian swimmer Duke Kahanamoku had a small part as a pirate captain. Hugo Riesenfeld and an associate named Zamecknik arranged the musical score for the pit orchestra.

Probably because of Grauman's preoccupation with the Chinese Theater's construction in late 1926, a deal fell through that might have altered Sid's career. Grauman and Joseph M. Schenck were good friends through many years. In 1926 they visited New York with the tentative plan to build a chain of thirteen new theaters around the United States, all houses to be patterned after the Egyptian. This deal was never consummated, and it probably was a good thing, since had it been, Grauman might not have been able to lavish the peak of his creative energies on the golden years of the world's most famous movie palace, the Chinese

The Duncan Sisters, Rosetta and Vivian, accept the key to the city of Los Angeles from Mayor George Cryer (1927).

The overture was a "Way Down South" medley, with Bakaleinikoff conducting and Frederick Burr Scholl at the Wurlitzer. The scene of the Prologue was a plantation house on the Mississippi, replete "with Jubilee Singers, Pickaninny Dancers [and there were no pickets at the box office], Plantation Instrumentalists, and Southern Belles." The principal entertainers and specialty acts were all listed by name in the program and set the scene for the "internationally famed and beloved" Duncan Sisters who had written new songs for their Hollywood appearance at the Egyptian. The program had a note explaining that the Duncans would be seen in their personal programs of old and new songs and comedy at every performance during the run of the picture. *Topsy and Eva* on film was an extremely lightweight tour de force, but the rowdy Duncan Sisters in person more than made up for it; they were a sensation.

The bill at the Egyptian was in dramatic contrast to the presentation at the recently opened Chinese Theater. A month earlier Grauman's newest house had premiered *King of Kings*, which immediately became the most distinguished film of the year, greatly enhanced by its sumptuous Prologue with two hundred people onstage. But at the Egyptian Theater in his last personally supervised program, Grauman went a bit overboard. The entire cast of *Topsy and Eva*, the Prologue, along with the usherettes, footmen, doormen, and all theater attaches, were assembled by Grauman for an elaborate dress rehearsal to ensure a flawless farewell world premiere performance. Director Fred Niblo was emcee once more on June 16, introducing the *Topsy and Eva* cast, and then the Prologue with a cast of fifty artists.

"It's a show at any rate," Schallert wrote in the *Times* a few days after the opening, "that much may definitely be set forth. . . . The youngsters will probably enjoy it most. Rosetta and Vivian Duncan were tendered a huge reception at the premiere (with that bright interest and sparkle that usually surrounds a Grauman opening. . . .) The Duncan Sisters . . . are popular idols. They sang familiar numbers and new ones, and they looked more than attractive when they came on stage wearing blond wigs and Rosetta minus her blackface make-up."

The Prologue was almost as long as the feature itself. "A picture largely of gags," Schallert called it, "to which the plot, what there is of it, seems en-

Theater. Ads were already calling the Egyptian Theater "A Mecca for Tourists" and "The World's Most Picturesque Playhouse" while *Old Ironsides* was playing there. New adjectives would have to be invented to cope with the exotic splendor of the Chinese.

The last feature to play the Egyptian Theater under the long-run policy was *Topsy and Eva* with the Duncan Sisters, vaudeville's top female sibling comedy act of the late 1920s. No one knew better than Grauman that the Duncans had to be seen in person to be properly appreciated, so to make their screen debut in the outrageous film takeoff of *Uncle Tom's Cabin*, which was called *Topsy and Eva*, Grauman presented the sisters onstage in his and choreographer Larry Ceballos's Prologue called "Plantation Memories" set in the pre-Civil War South.

tirely incidental. . . . Were it made with anybody but the Duncan Sisters as stars it would have to be rated as a very poor picture. . . . The Grauman prologue includes various specialty performers who scored remarkable individual hits. Taken all in all, the show is entertaining."

Louella O. Parsons called Rosetta Duncan "a female Charlie Chaplin in black-face. . . . Rosetta is a discovery. . . . I was so delighted with [her] Al Jolson stuff that I have to say, Rosetta is to the screen what Al Jolson is to the stage, a black-face artist without equal . . . . The Duncans and Sid Grauman are a great trio. The girls furnish sparkling comedy and Sid offers the Graumanesque touch, now recognized as the Tiffany of showmanship. Certainly he took advantage of the 'Way-Down-South' notion by giving us a generous measure of plantation life [old mansion, etc.]. . . . The prologue, mind you, lasted an hour and ten minutes, an evening's entertainment in itself. . . ."

Parsons's observation brings up an interesting point. Why didn't Sid concentrate in his early professional years entirely on stage production and turn his back on the movies? Film was not considered respectable until D. W. Griffith (who, incidentally, staged a beautiful and significant Prologue to *The Greatest Things in Life* at Clune's Auditorium before the Million Dollar Theater opened). Yet Sid, with only minor excursions into legitimate theater, stuck to exhibiting all through his career, with the Prologues as mere adjuncts to the films. Sid may have privately considered stage productions inferior by the standards of the legitimate theater. If so, this was probably because he was hopelessly film-struck, and not stagestruck. He needed the stimulus of films to produce his stage shows and used them as ornamentation for the films exhibited. Even with the thin fare that *Topsy and Eva* offered, Sid made the picture look better through a hit Prologue, a delightful entertainment in which the Duncans scored a great personal triumph over the footlights at every performance.

Topsy and Eva proved to be a most joyful vehicle through which Sid could terminate his impressive tenure at the Egyptian. At the end of the show's brief run, the theater went dark on July 20, 1927. It opened a couple of days later under new West Coast Theater management, with a continuous performance policy at popular prices, and no Grauman Prologue ever graced its stage again, sadly enough.

11

AN indication of Sid's theatrical intentions appeared as a note in the March 14, 1925, issue of *Motion Picture News* with the banner headline SCHENCK AND GRAUMAN TO BUILD FIRST RUN HOUSES: "Joseph M. Schenck announced in Los Angeles last week that he and Sid would build a chain of ten or fifteen first runs across the country. Obviously these will be primarily an outlet for United Artists pictures."

Schenck's announcement caused widespread speculation in the theater world, and some discussion as to whether the first of the theater chain's houses would be built in New York.

"Sid and I will furnish part of the capital," Schenck said, "and the rest will be handled by Blair & Company of Wall Street." (This was a procedure similar to the one the two men had followed in other business dealings.) We plan to erect three of the ten or fifteen theaters at an early date. The first will be in New York on a site yet to be definitely determined. We are negotiating, however, for a Broadway property further down than the Strand Theater."

Prior to this announcement, it was stated that Schenck and Grauman were to build a $2,000,000 theater in Los Angeles. In connection with Schenck's statement about the theater chain, it was noted that Grauman, upon his return from Europe, had told newsmen that he would build a theater in New York at a cost of about $5 million, modeled after the Egyptian Theater in Hollywood, the design of all the chain theaters to be the same.

A few months before the Schenck-Grauman plans were made public, Sid was in New York. On August 6, 1924, he sailed on the *Leviathan* for a stay of several months in Europe. Before sailing Sid told *Motion Picture News* that he had plans in mind that might result in the building of a Grauman theater in Paris and also one in London. These plans never materialized, but they were indications that something was in genesis. That something was ultimately the illustrious Grauman's Chinese Theater, in its prime the most spectacular house anywhere in the world—and even now, after its fiftieth anniversary, the most famous movie house, attracting more than two million patrons and visitors within its unique Oriental pagoda walls each year. Pilgrims come from everywhere to view the hand and footprints of Hollywood's immortals as they were impressed into the forecourt concrete. Others come to sit in the beautiful auditorium, not as handsome as it originally was but still unique, and absorb the exotic atmosphere of this veritable temple to cinema.

The building of the Chinese Theater was the supreme achievement of Sid Grauman, known among his peers as "the P. T. Barnum of the movies." Since he first packaged the combination of live shows and films, it was Sid's continuing dream to build a truly magnificent motion picture house that would eventually become world famous. The Million Dollar Theater was a step in that direction, the Egyptian Theater another move toward Sid's goal, and the Chinese Theater the ultimate realization, which went beyond even Grauman's most expansive dreams.

Ten days before the May 18, 1927, opening of the Chinese Theater the *Examiner* was calling it a theater of ultramandarin architecture, and pointed out that the house had already received international recognition for its superb decor. Inspected by students of Chinese art, government officials, and businessmen, all declared the Chinese to be faithful to Chinese architecture. Actually it was a combination of many styles of classic Oriental art that had been brought into high theatrical synthesis by Grauman and his building associates. The structure was luxuriously appointed, rich in color and form, ornate and yet somehow unified, its accoutrement the best and the latest that money could buy. Even before the grand opening the Chinese had become a Los Angeles semicivic institution (now listed as one of the city's prime historical landmarks), for word-of-mouth publicity about its exterior and interior beauty from other architects described the Chinese as the world's most exquisite jewel of a playhouse.

Tirelessly insistent on absolute top quality throughout during the construction of the Chinese, Grauman not only passed on all the major aspects of the house but on just about every single small detail—down to light switches and the laying of tiles. He personally designed the stage, the largest used by any motion picture house anywhere. All twenty-two hundred seats were set on a continuously raked floor plan, the pitch of the auditorium rising to meet the ground-level lobby, so that all patrons, even those in the extreme rear side seats, could enjoy a comprehensive and unimpeded view of all parts of the house. This architectural detail had served Grauman well in the construction of the Million Dollar, Metropolitan, and Egyptian theaters.

Grauman and his staff of architects and builders studied the floor plans of more than two hundred theaters built in the five years previous to the Chinese before a single sketch was made for the house. Some twenty thousand photographs of Chinese art and architecture were carefully examined for the elaborate detail work that was involved. This exhaustive preparation paid off, for even today, with certain original features gone from the inside and outside of the venerable theater, its homogenous beauty remains its outstanding charm, even though the forecourt footprints get most of the attention by the mass of visitors.

The best features of houses in Europe and in North and South America were incorporated into the design of the final plan. These were augmented by the special theatrical features that Sid Grauman had worked out in his various Los Angeles houses since the building of the Million Dollar Theater, and the final result was little short of awesome. There had been bigger and more expensive houses, but none anywhere that balanced all the features found in the Chinese in such total harmony. The house was as functional as it was beautiful, and so it remains today.

"The Chinese was so designed," said the *Examiner*, "that great spectacles, grand opera or, in fact, any form of entertainment may be presented. The theater represents Sid Grauman's dream of years to erect a theater magnificent enough to become a byword throughout the world. Viewing the playhouse from across Hollywood Boulevard at Orchid Avenue, one sees a towering pagoda, typically Chinese, beneath which lie the main entrances. Before the pagoda is a courtyard with palms and tropical plants. Fountains decorate each side wall of the curved courtyard, and two large coco palms are set."

As in China, the theater's roof is the building's chief feature; it draws the eye immediately as one stands before the facade. Supported by two huge, octagonal pillars, the great central entrance tower at the forecourt's rear sends its multiroofed, bronze green pagoda skyward. The jagged eaves tilt up like forked dragon tongues. An actual dragon climbs vertically up the recessed front center panel of the tower, a yellow emblem attesting to the power of the spirit, an effect generally worked into the color spectrum of Chinese temples and palaces.

On both sides of the main entrance doors stand Chinese heaven dogs of stone, first seen in Chinese art in the second century B. C. These are meant to ward off evil spirits and are authentic Chinese im-

Grauman's Chinese Theater in Hollywood: the main house curtain (1927).

ports of antique vintage. Minor towers project at regular intervals from the top of the great curved forecourt wall. High up on the wall are lighting fixtures that shed soft colored lights on shrubbery and palms. The wall tops are ornamented with dwarf shrubs. Silhouetted against the day or night sky, the shrubs complete the temple garden effect of the courtyard. Each detail was Sid Grauman's final choice, and even today these reflect the careful thought and deep sense of harmony that Sid managed to achieve by the skillful coordination of highly disparate elements.

The foyer of the Chinese, says a 1938 brochure, displayed a king's ransom in art treasures imported from China. The carpets were thick and beautifully designed; tapestries and pictures adorned the walls, with occasional recessed shrines and altars and wax figures of startling reality in sumptuous Oriental robes. The intricate glass and metal chandeliers cast diffused, varicolored light on the tall vases and urns, which were authentic Chinese mandarin acquisitions.

Among the foyer treasures (in 1938) there remained an unusual painting entitled *Hollywood Comes to Napoleon's Aid*, which depicted Napoleon and his staff after the victory at Austerlitz. The generals were recognizable motion picture celebrities, painted by a self-taught thirteen-year-old Hollywood artist, Charles De Ravenne, who spent three years on the work valued at $25,000. Background characters in the painting included Erich Von Stroheim, Douglas Fairbanks, Clive Brook, Adolphe Menjou, Sid Grauman, Joseph Schenck, William Powell, Charles Chaplin, and Marion Davies. Sid was apparently fond of joking that the painting was a "genuine antique" item.

Grauman's Chinese Theater: view of auditorium from stage (1927).

It was not, of course, and has long since disappeared.

During Grauman's tenure, the Chinese Theater was always delicately scented with essence of sandalwood, creating the hushed and heady atmosphere of an ancient Chinese temple. The lavish ceiling of ivory, gold, red, and black, its pendant crystals, looked like the interior of a Chinese jewel box. Even the orchestra lights in the pit were Chinese lanterns on stands that changed color during the overture. Afterwards, the entire auditorium would be revealed in a blaze of white crystals and pearls, illuminating the true colors of the interior.

The Chinese-cabinet asbestos fire curtain was in view when patrons entered the house before a performance. It was a deep peacock blue, with human figures and trees in bronze, seemingly three-dimensional. The gradual slow rise of the curtain made it a spectacle not to be missed, with Sid's favorite organ solo, "Pomp and Circumstance," resounding through the house.

The Wurlitzer organ console of ebony decorated with floral designs in gold stood at the extreme right in the orchestra pit, balanced by a fake console on the left side. The Wurlitzer's loft was directly over the stage proscenium, with sonic outlets through the central chandelier grilles. Although it was not as effective as a similar arrangement at the Egyptian Theater, the music did seem to float down upon the audience from some celestial source, as Hollywood expert Terry Helgesen points out in his *Console* magazine brochure on the Chinese. In 1958, the beautiful Wurlitzer 3M/17R was removed from its stationary pit location in the Chi-

108

Grauman's Chinese Theater in Hollywood: the final stages of construction.

Interior of auditorium of Grauman's Chinese Theater (1927).

nese and donated by the theater chain to St. Finbar's Catholic Church in Burbank, where it was revoiced for sacred music.

The stage of the Chinese Theater was enormous in proportion to the house's seating capacity; 165 feet wide and 48 feet deep, with a massive and sophisticated switchboard to the audience's left backstage. The very latest in projector equipment was operated from the central mezzanine projector booth, giving the large audience a fine picture wherever patrons were seated.

Working with Grauman on house details was architect Raymond Kennedy, who was responsible for much of the glory that is (or was) the Chinese Theater. Kennedy worked for the firm of Meyer and Holler, the theater's builders, who have always been credited with the overall design of the cinema temple. Terry Helgesen interviewed Kennedy in his Glendale, California, home within recent years and viewed the original sketches and design detail for the Chinese, executed in black and white drawings.

"Many have said in the past," states Helgesen, "that Grauman's Chinese Theater was not authentically Chinese, architecturally or decoratively, and it has been pointed out that the Fifth Avenue Theater in Seattle, which opened a year before the Chinese, was designed much more in the traditional architectural style of that far east country [than Grauman's Chinese was]. This is perfectly true, but what Mr. Kennedy had done was to take his inspiration from the Chinese period of Chippendale, rather than the heavier feeling one would get from the actual architecture of China, and indeed, it couldn't have been done more gracefully."

Architect Kennedy was responsible for the two ornate metal and crystal pagodas that flanked each side of the great stage. After the screen began to talk in 1929, sound vibrations from the speakers caused the pagodas to flutter and give off an audible tinkling sound. This so disturbed patrons that finally the pagodas were reluctantly removed. Kennedy followed the suggestions of Sid Grauman, of Meyer and Holler, the architect-engineers, and his own professional training in the formulation of the plans for the Chinese Theater. Eventually, as the theater aged, many of the singular original features were removed, including the great stage, the chandelier, the organ, and many other glamorous and ornamental features. The projection room was removed from the central mezzanine and located at the rear center of the main floor, blocking off the central auditorium doors. When the original carpets were worn out, copies of these beautiful works were substituted, and some decorative painting was done to refresh the house. But the auditorium had lost its original glory; no amount of restoration will ever reinstill that.

For anyone who knew the theater in the splendid prime of those first years of Grauman long runs, and lucky enough to see its initial bill, *King of Kings*, with its glorious Prologue, and who is able to recall the breathtaking beauties of the house and performance, it is depressing to dwell on what once was and certainly can never be again. It is enough to state once more that Ted Mann, the current owner, has attempted in all good conscience to preserve what is left of the Grauman monument and has built his new two additional smaller houses, the Chinese II and Chinese III, next door to the famous landmark instead of restructuring the still-lovely interior of the house.

Of all the Grauman opening nights, May 18,

1927, may have been the grandest. The *Times* reported that spectators, the famous and the merely ticket-lucky, sat hushed before the magnificence of the Christ story. Schallert called the film dignified and tenderly reverential in the spirit of its interpretation, and rich in dramatic inspiration. De Mille's production was quite remote from the ordinary realms of entertainment. During the making of the film, De Mille had kept H. B. Warner (who played Christ) under wraps and the sets shrouded in secrecy, since many Fundamentalists decried the human portrayal of Christ on film, which had never before been attempted.

"As an event, the first unfolding of *King of Kings* on the screen took precedence even over the opening of a theater that in itself is a revelation of art and beauty," Schallert declared. "Grauman's Chinese Theater is the ultimate word in construction and imagination. . . . Triumphant also was the premiere. . . . It is a strange anomaly, of course, that makes the first showing of the picture telling the Christ story incidental to the opening of a theater that in its ultimate fulfillment will be dedicated purely to entertainment, and a Chinese theater in particular. Many might have been inclined to find this circumstance an incongruity. And that such does exist cannot be denied. . . ." There was, however, much praise eventually from the religious leaders of Los Angeles for the dignity with which De Mille presented his masterpiece and for the continuous reverence with which Grauman staged his ambitious Prologue with its cast of some two hundred.

"The Prologue adheres to a fine simplicity," said Schallert.

Much of it is in tableau form and much is given over to choruses [of sacred music]. There is also singing during the musical score by Hugo Riesenfeld, which score is itself a surpassing achievement. A harp ensemble is an effective musical addition. . . . The manger tableau, the flight into Egypt, the coming of The Three Wise Men across the desert, and the final dazzling transformations aiming at a celestial glamour, all add to the presentation, which truly exerts a rare and exceptional spell over its audience. . . .

A word more with reference to the theater itself. No prophet is needed to foretell the future of this picturesque establishment. Sid Grauman has a home for the productions that he will henceforth show there whose fame will become international. The house is a dream of beauty in both lighting and decorative effects—an Aladdin

Advertisement for May 18, 1927.

111

wonder palace that will be seen by all who visit Southern California, or dwell here, as an institution. . . .

If the "Hollywood" premiere was an event of importance when Grauman staged them at the Million Dollar, Rialto, and Egyptian performances, the premiere reached new brilliance at Grauman's Chinese Theater. Although the *King of Kings* premiere had its moments of reverent lip service to a solemn subject and a gorgeous cinema temple, it nevertheless attracted a huge and demonstrative street crowd, which, considering its vast numbers, behaved well enough. On November 4, 1927, six months after the Chinese opened, and four months after the Egyptian passed out of Grauman's management, Sid premiered the second Chinese feature, starring Douglas Fairbanks in *The Gaucho*, an adventure film with the Black Death and a miracle built into it, an offbeat tale that was perhaps the most atmospheric feature that Fairbanks ever made. It showed the athletic star in an entirely new mien, making him much more sedate, said Louella O. Parsons.

"Hollywood's sorcerer, that amazingly dynamic and creative Sid Grauman, last night staged another of his extraordinary premieres," said Louella in the following day's *Examiner*.

This time he had Douglas Fairbanks and his latest film . . . as the basis for his theatrical activities. But it wasn't any more Doug than Sid. Alone either one can command a crowd of film celebrities—together they are an unbeatable combination. . . . A Grauman opening always means so much more than just the feature picture, we usually admit grudgingly, and jealously watch so that the prologue does not steal any of the glory of the motion picture. There could be no such feeling in this Grauman prologue. . . . Mr. Grauman is showing enough to build his effects with the theme of the picture in mind. . . . What Mr. Grauman did in a brief week with the South American locale adds new laurels to his reputation as a showman. That Argentine music. . . . Borrah Minnevitch—yes, the name is Russian but the music is harmonically rendered by an orchestra [all harmonica players] of all ages and sizes of boy. Mr. Minnevitch's direction and comedy . . . no one should miss. Samuel Pedraza . . . a voice that calls immediately for an encore, and Harry A. White and Alice Manning in a dance number, are all headliners in a complete vaudeville entertainment. The indivi-

dual performances with a background of sparkling senoritas, dashing Argentine youth and uniformed soldiers, . . . occupied more than an hour.

The Gaucho offers a new Doug, a less volatile, a less agile and more sedate young man. The old glamour of his smile, his famous jumps and his escapades with the gentle ladies . . . [are] somewhat subdued by the religious tone of the story.

In the *Times*, Schallert said that Douglas Fairbanks managed to slip away to New York upon nearly every previous occasion when one of his pictures opened in Hollywood, and most of these played the East Coast before showing in California. "Breaking the precedent," said Schallert, "was the signal for practically every celebrity in the film world to appear, and [give] a notable ovation for Doug himself when he appeared on stage in the course of the inaugural ceremonies."

Conrad Nagel was the emcee at the premiere, introducing Fairbanks and newcomer Lupe Velez, the Latin spitfire from the film who went on to become a star in her own right. Schallert lauded the stage show for its sterling entertainment values and commended Doug on his serious film and Grauman on another superior Prologue.

On January 29, 1928, Schallert reviewed Charlie Chaplin's *The Circus* at the Chinese: "Chaplin won proof last evening of the devotion of Hollywood and compensated the premiere audience for his picture *The Circus* with one of his most triumphant achievements. . . . A festive opening was celebrated by Sid Grauman in token of the stellar comedian's first production since *The Gold Rush. The Circus* is a show for everybody . . . and so too is the prologue, in which Poodles Hanneford [clown supreme] does some uproarious entertaining . . . ."

Grauman staged an elaborate one-ring circus under a canvas top on the mammoth stage. Arthur Kay conducted the orchestra and opened with a lively overture, "A Trip to the Side Show." The acts included the Three Freehands, acrobats; Samaroff and Sonia, dancers; Famous Cloudburst; Pepito the Clown; Fallenger's Bears; Ed and Jenny Rooney; and Poodles.

"Sid's prologue," said Schallert, "is a perfect show for kiddies. Hanneford is a star second only to Charlie. What with performing bears, a dazzling aerial artist, remarkable acrobats and tumblers . . . there is no end of interest . . . Just before the picture, Fred Niblo introduced Chaplin, Merna Kennedy, Harry Crocker [and other members] of *The Circus* cast. Charlie received a notable ovation." In the first three stellar attractions to play the Chinese Theater, Grauman had distinguished himself as a showman of legendary proportions, second to none in the West.

12

THE fourth attraction at the Chinese Theater was the May 7, 1928, opening of a spectacular adventure film called *The Trail of '98*, with Dolores Del Rio, Karl Dane, Ralph Forbes, Harry Carey, and Tully Marshall. The film was a vivid portrayal of the gold trek of 1898 to Alaska, a subject as familiar to Grauman as was Chaplin's *The Gold Rush*, and Sid gave it a brilliant setting. Although the film offered exciting visual effects, such as the shooting of the White Horse Rapids, the real innovation was a new device, the so-called wide "Fantom" screen.

In the *Times*, Schallert said that the screen proved very effective in the slick transition from the stage Prologue to the film by eliminating the dropping of the curtain between the two divisions of the program. The Alaskan dance hall set on which the Prologue was staged was made in two movable sections. At the finale these portions were wheeled apart to give a gradually enlarging view of the motion picture screen in the background. "As the two platforms moved offstage, one to the right wing and the other to the left, respectively, the title of *The Trail of '98* began to appear on the screen with aurora-borealis lighting effects, then by degrees the screen itself moved forward to its normal position in relation to the audience." The picture credits then began to unreel. Clarence

Brown's feature was greatly enhanced by the Prologue, and the bill played into June.

In an article by Louella O. Parsons in the *Examiner* of July 29, 1928, the doyenne of Hollywood columnists discussed Grauman's plans for the Chinese Theater. "After being closed for over five long weeks, Grauman's Chinese Theater, a mecca for tourists from all over the world, will reopen Friday night, August 3rd. Grauman has selected Metro-Goldwyn-Mayer's first sound motion picture, *White Shadows in the South Seas*, to be the featured attraction. It is produced in the new Movietone process. The actual sound track is on the film alongside the photo frame [instead of being a synchronized disc, such as Vitaphone first was]. The new film stars Monte Blue and Raquel Torres. Grauman plans on presenting an elaborate stage prologue to the feature. . . ."

There was some serious theater competition for Grauman that August. The Metropolitan Theater screened its first talking picture on August 10, a Warner Brothers Vitaphone feature called *Caught in the Fog*, with May McAvoy, Conrad Nagel, and Mack Swain, plus a big Publix Stage Revue from New York with comedian George Givot. On August 25, the Shrine Civic Auditorium opened as a movie house. With a seating capacity of six thousand, the Shrine was easily the world's largest photoplay palace. All seats were twenty-five cents, and the double bill was Marion Davies in *The Fair Coed* and Edmund Lowe in *Dressed to Kill*, with the added attraction of a new cool air ventilating system. In downtown Los Angeles the United Artists Theater was showing its first sound picture, Victor Hugo's novel, *The Man Who Laughs*, with Conrad Veidt and Mary Philbin. Warner Brothers Hollywood Theater was showing its first all-talking thriller, *The Terror*, with comedienne Louise Fazenda, Edward Everett Horton, and May McAvoy. The newly renovated Criterion Theater in downtown Los Angeles reopened on August 18 with Fox-Movietone's sound film, *Street Angel*, starring the romantic team of Charles Farrell and Janet Gaynor. Bakaleinikoff conducted the twenty-piece Criterion Orchestra.

White Shadows opened the Chinese Theater on August 3, 1928, accompanied by a Prologue called "The Tropics." An added extra bonus was Marveltone Talking Pictures. "Folks fought to get in," said J. M. Loughborough in *Exhibitors Herald*, at a Sid Grauman premiere that was more Graumanesque than ever. The performance had a lot of publicity and a five dollar top. "A platoon of police was kept busy all evening to hold the curious ones in check. . . . It was a magnificent affair in every way, this premiere, which also marked the reopening of the Chinese and likewise the debut of Sid Grauman as an exhibitor in the field of the talkies. . . ." Apparently the early Vitaphone scoop with *Don Juan* at the Egyptian two years earlier did not count as a full-fledged entry into the field of sound pictures.

Sid appeared as an actor in films for the first time on the *White Shadows* bill. "A short Movietone [featurette] served to introduce the stars of the big production, Monte Blue and Raquel Torres," said Loughborough, "and the director Wm. S. Van Dyke. In this same film Grauman acted as master of ceremonies [momentarily, not actually playing a role]. Sid proved that he is as much actor as he is good scout. Talkie producers would do well to keep an eye on him. Faultlessly attired, his hair looking like Paderewski's did 20 years ago, Grauman swept out from behind plush curtains, faced the audience with a Fairbanks smile and a Conrad Nagel voice, and announced the appearance of Monte Blue. Monte movietoned front and center, and introduced Van Dyke. Then came

Raquel. . . ." (Raquel Torres, incidentally, was among the usherettes who worked the opening of the Chinese. A year later she was an actress. Sid wanted to incorporate her prints in the forecourt of the Chinese, but MGM refused, since they had given out the publicity that she was practically kidnapped from a Mexican convent by the movies.) "There were many surprising bits of showmanship in connection with *White Shadows*," Loughborough continues,

but as Pete Smith of MGM was in evidence in the lobby, he and Grauman get the credit.

For instance, there was a battery of motion picture cameras, sent by MGM. Directed by James Cruze, the cameraman took pictures of the stars, who turned out with more brilliancy than any stellar show to be seen on a clear night at Mount Wilson Observatory. Also, there were other celebrities. The popular O. O. McIntyre [celebrated Hearst columnist and national wit] rolled up in his new Rolls Royce and looked more like a production executive than a journalist. The eyes of "Once Over" were full of fire, and he acted like a kid. Milt Gross, the "Nize Baby" cartoon boy, also came forward, giving the reminder of how Chaplin looked at Milt's age. Irene Rich was so full of fun and pep that she actually did a bit of feminine "clowning" before the camera. Director Van Dyke entered the frame with David Wark Griffith. Louis B. Mayer appeared with his charming wife and their handsome daughters. L. B. looked proud, but he walked in meekly, dodging both radio microphone and camera. Most of the notables spoke over the radio, which was in charge of Fred Niblo. . . .

Fox Movietone News, which opened the show, included a sound sequence of a huge army tank mowing down a forest that Loughborough called awe-inspiring. Sid's South Sea Prologue followed, featuring the Brox Sisters, Kenneth Olds, Hawaiian dancers, and a troupe of Samoan chieftains.

White Shadows concerned Dr. Lloyd, a white physician played by Monte Blue, a human derelict on a South Sea island. There were fine shots of natives diving for pearls, encounters with sharks, an octopus, and the intrusion of the white traders, who resent the doctor and decide to kidnap him. They lash him to the mast of a ship carrying the dead victims of bubonic plague which sails into a typhoon. Dr. Lloyd is shipwrecked on an island Garden of Eden, hailed as a god by the childlike natives. He marries a lovely island girl, played by

Raquel Torres. All is idyllic until Lloyd's old trader enemy appears and decides to set up headquarters on the island. Lloyd starts a fight and is shot and killed. The Samoan bride loses her god, a sad but logical ending to a really marvelous sound picture, for its time. Loughborough said, "One feels that all other pictures dealing with primitive peoples have been far overshadowed; that this is something which puts Flaherty's mighty *Nanook of the North* into the background." This wasn't quite the verdict of the future, but in the early days of sound, reviewers were often overcome with praise at the successful combination of audiovisual images.

The *White Shadows* bill offered a varied and exciting program. Movietone shorts, one with comedians Clark and McCullough, proved emphatically that sound entertainment had caught popular fancy and was here to stay. The Chinese Theater closed *White Shadows* on October 21, and was dark for the second time that year. On November 1, 1928, Grauman opened the house again with the Warner Brothers production of *Noah's Ark*, a feeble attempt at a biblical theme that fell uncomfortably short of both *The Ten Commandments* and *King of Kings*.

Terry Helgesen, in his memorial brochure on the Chinese Theater, discusses the merits of the Chinese Wurlitzer organ and relates an incident in which the skill of organist Frank Lanterman carried the inept *Noah's Ark* epic right into the Chinese Theater.

Lanterman said that he played the Chinese Wurlitzer only once, at a special preview showing of *Noah's Ark* for Sid Grauman and his staff after the regular theater performance late one night. Jack Warner hired Lanterman to come over from the Alex Theater in Glendale to play the film. Warner knew that the picture was a failure and told Lanterman so privately. With members from the Alex staff to man the thundersheet and two tympani, and Lanterman hitting the heavy pedal ranks on the organ at strategic points to intensify screen action, Grauman was so impressed that he booked the picture, or so the story goes. "This was a case where a complete disaster of a picture was pulled out of total failure by a Wurlitzer," said Lanterman.

Noah's Ark, which had a script by Darryl Zanuck and was directed by Michael Curtiz, starred Dolores Costello, George O'Brien, Noah Beery, and

Louise Fazenda. Like *The Ten Commandments*, it contained two stories, ancient and modern, with the cast doubling roles. The picture was notable for its musical score and the Vitaphone Symphony Orchestra conducted by Louis Silvers, and for the almost invisible Myrna Loy as a slave girl and a modern dancer.

Sid presented his atmospheric conception as a prelude to the film, with a male chorus singing "Hear My Prayer" with Stewart Brady, now billed as the Boy Tenor. There were pictorial tableaux—"Christ before Pilate" and "The Last Supper" followed by a picturesque tableau of "Noah's Ark." The mixed chorus sang again, this time "Unfold Ye Portals" from Gounod's *Redemption*. Movietone News and other talking picture subjects were introduced before the film. The Prologue was short and colorful; wisely so, because the film was dull and interminable. *Noah's Ark* closed on January 16, 1929, after a ten-week run.

Two weeks later, on February 1, 1929, Grauman opened the Chinese Theater with the MGM musical *Broadway Melody*, starring the New York musical comedy star Charles King, Anita Page, and diminutive Bessie Love. It was a backstage-success, tears-and-laughter tale of two sisters. The critics nationwide were quick to laud the picture as the finest talkie yet to come out of Hollywood. The public responded with similar approval and made it a resounding hit. Starring in Sid Grauman's Prologue were the Broadway team of Buster and John West, recent stars of George White's Scandals, the Albertina Rasch Ballet, Alfred Catell, the Pasquali Brothers, Jerry Coe, and others.

Louella O. Parsons said in the *Examiner*: "With *Broadway Melody* as a working basis, Sid Grauman just had to outdo himself. He hasn't had such a winner pictorially or in his prologue since *The Circus*. What a revue he offers! It's an entire entertainment in itself. The chorus with eighty-four beautiful girls would do credit to either George White or Flo Ziegfeld. . . . Yes, Sid is back in his old stride. . . ."

That same week an *Examiner* headline said that RESERVE BANKS HIT STOCK GAMBLING, which was buying on margin, a common practice in 1929. Also, a permit was issued to build the New Pantages Theater on Hollywood Boulevard just east of Vine Street at a cost of $2.9 million. Warner Brothers was planning another theater to be located near its Hollywood house. Fox announced building plans for a new $10 million theater in downtown Los Angeles, although the exact site was not announced.

On June 20, 1929, Grauman held the world premiere of MGM's *Hollywood Revue of 1929*, called the greatest musical ever produced, although it is remembered today mainly for the song "Singin' in the Rain." The film crowded almost the entire roster of studio stars into its cast and gave them voices with varying degrees of appeal. A few days before the opening of the *Hollywood Revue*, an item in the *Examiner* contained important news. Sid was leasing the Chinese Theater to Fox West Coast Theater Corporation. Sid did not disclose any plans for his future in the theater business, although it was rumored that he might go into the production of talking pictures for the United Artists Corporation. At the same time that *The Hollywood Revue of 1929* opened, Fox West Coast Theaters' general manager H. B. Franklin announced the appointment of Rusty White as the new manager of the Chinese; he had been transferred from downtown Loew's State for the job. Almost immediately a new policy was inaugurated at the Chinese. A Billion Dollar Midnight Matinee was to be held each Saturday night with "the largest jazz band in the world, with 40 syncoposts led by Rube Wolf, in addition to 30 symphonists—" as the ad stated. MGM stars (mostly young featured players) sometimes appeared in person at these performances.

The famous Grauman theme Prologues that had prefaced feature pictures at the Chinese Theater since its opening were terminated with the departure of Sid. Although the Chinese Theater continued to screen many distinguished features, Sid was still out of the theater business at the end of 1929.

In January 1930, Metropolitan Opera baritone Lawrence Tibbett appeared in *The Rogue Song*, the MGM musical romance that also featured Laurel and Hardy, with a stage show by Abe Lyman and his orchestra. "The Kit Kat Club Revue" was patterned after an evening at the famous London nitery, but it had nothing to do with the feature. Fox West Coast Theaters had soon discovered that the Chinese Theater did not draw nearly as well without some kind of tandem live presentation, even if it were unrelated to the feature picture.

On February 26, 1930, Sid returned briefly to the scene of his first Los Angeles triumphs, the Million Dollar Theater, as the guest of honor to help formalize the opening of a new Tiffany Picture,

Party Girl. This was one of two public appearances that Grauman made right after his retirement from the Chinese. The master showman obviously was not considering total withdrawal from the public eye.

On May 22, 1930, a surprise item in the *Examiner* announced that Sid would return to the Chinese Theater. He signed a contract with Fox West Coast Theaters to manage the house and to produce the famous Grauman Prologues once again. This was good news for entertainment professionals and brought a lot of free newspaper publicity to the Chinese, especially since the film chosen for Grauman's return was considered a blockbuster even before its release; it had been made by a young tycoon who had arranged for Grauman's return.

The widely discussed world premiere took place on May 27, 1930. The feature was Howard Hughes's long-anticipated, precedent-breaking *Hell's Angels*, starring Ben Lyon, James Hall, and Jean Harlow, the platinum-haired beauty in the role that sent her on to stardom. Reserved seats were an astronomical eleven dollars and the ads promised that one thousand movie stars would appear at the Chinese Theater for the event. There would also be the greatest outdoor show ever presented, in the skies over Hollywood Boulevard. The air would be filled with searchlights, airplanes in mock battle, fireworks, and more. The advertising brought out a crowd estimated at very near 150,000. A near-riot ensued and the police had all they could do to keep the mob in check, so eager were those attending the arrival of limousines at the theater. (It has been suggested that novelist Nathanael West based the premiere scenes in *Day of the Locust* on this particular evening.) Grauman's Prologue was called "more stupendous than a New York stage revue," with Mitchell and Durant, the Albertina Rasch Ballet girls, and several other sterling acts. It was not, however, among his best.

By September 22, 1930, Sid was reported to be leaving his post at the Chinese Theater. Newspaper ads dropped the trademark name of Prologue from their billing, substituting the term Gigantic Stage Revue. A few days later *Hell's Angels* closed, and special equipment was installed in the theater to show the new Grandeur Film on a giant screen.

The world premiere of Fox's *The Big Trail*, directed by Raoul Walsh and starring the then-unknown John Wayne, featured El Brendel, Mar-

World premiere of Howard Hughes's *Hell's Angels*, starring Jean Harlow, James Hall, and Ben Lyon. Approximately 150,000 fans lined Hollywood Boulevard from the Chinese Theater to Hollywood and Vine to watch the approach of the stars attending the opening.

Jean Harlow and Ben Lyon in a scene from Howard Hughes's production of *Hell's Angels*.

guerite Churchill, Tully Marshall, and a cast of twenty thousand, many of which were buffalo. Numerous publicity gimmicks were tried out at the Chinese in Grauman's various absences, but nothing worked as well as the theme Prologues had with their companion films. One publicity stunt projected in 1930 was the installation of a novel Curtain of Stars created by musician/artist Xavier Cugat. The curtain was forty by sixty feet in size, and depicted six-foot-tall movie stars. The curtain was previewed with Carli Elinor and an augmented symphony orchestra playing the appropriate medley of tunes as the stars were picked out by spotlight.

Jean Harlow, Ben Lyon, James Hall, and Evelyn Hall in a party scene from *Hell's Angels*.

The Chinese Theater, by virtue of its opulent Graumanesque originality, continued to be a favored house for pictures that demanded the glamour of a Hollywood premiere to showcase their arrival. After *The Big Trail*, Marlene Dietrich and Gary Cooper appeared there in *Morocco*, with a Prologue called "Moorish Melodic Panorama," conceived by Fanchon and Marco and staged by Larry Ceballos, with one hundred fifty people onstage and the Chinese Symphony Orchestra in the pit.

In January 1931, Sid ventured into legitimate theater production, presenting the West Coast company of the George S. Kauffman–Moss Hart hit, *Once in a Lifetime*, at the downtown Mayan Theater, a first-class legitimate theater with three stages. Florence Lawrence said of Grauman's production: "Long foremost in exposition of gigantic films, [Grauman] has demonstrated a showmanship which shows no limitations. He triumphed last

night in presenting this elaborate, fast-moving comedy before the footlights, as he has won again and again in the realm of silent and talking pictures." The comedy became a sound commercial success as screenland celebrities flocked to see the Hollywood satire and the general public came to see the stars. Next door to the Mayan at the smaller Belasco Theater, Leslie Howard and Margalo Gilmore were drawing large audiences to *Berkeley Square*. This was just the kind of associative "success breeds success" situation on which Sid thrived. His production played through to April.

On April 9, 1931, Sid offered a Graumanesque premiere to his next production, Elmer Rice's dynamic drama of New York City, *Street Scene*, with a New York cast of seventy-five. The production had some success with the critics and with the more discerning patrons, but it did not have wide appeal and closed in mid-May, to make way for Sid's production of the comedy, *Mrs. Bumpstead-Leigh*, starring Mrs. Minnie Maddern Fiske, a stage

Sid Grauman and Gail Patrick in *Mad about Music* **(1938).**

veteran. On June 19, 1931, Sid unveiled a production of the New York and London success, *The Man in Possession*, starring young Douglas Fairbanks, Jr., and the new MGM discovery, Nora Gregor.

"Manager Grauman programmed a show in front [of the Mayan] that was played by all those potent Hollywood stars," said Stevens of the *Examiner*, "to big searchlights, a sidewalk blocked with the curious and mobs of autograph questors." The show closed on July 21 after a comfortable run. The Mayan remained dark and Sid was once again out of the theater business.

Grauman made his return to the Chinese Theater on Christmas Day, 1931, with the premiere of MGM's *Hell Divers*, starring Clark Gable and Wallace Beery. A Prologue featured one hundred artists onstage, and the policy was two-a-day, with all seats reserved. Louella Parsons exulted about the event: "Sid Grauman is back! I would like to headline that in big letters because if anyone can coax Old Man Depression to fold up and depart, it's Hollywood's famous impresario. Good luck seems always to attend the Grauman premieres, largely because Sid never books a picture unless he personally believes in its entertainment qualities. He believes in *Hell Divers*. . . . Dear me, I realize I haven't said a word about the excellent Sid Grauman prologue. Well here is 'A Trip to a Mystic Land,' featuring several colorful numbers and the Chinese Augmented Symphony Orchestra conducted by Oscar Baum, with Perry Askam of the wonderful voice [the 1920s romantic singing lead

in the West Coast production of *The Desert Song*] and a male chorus of 20."

When *Grand Hotel* opened Grauman's Chinese Theater on April 29, 1932, a spectacular Prologue accompanied the movie. Even Grauman, however, could not lure Garbo to the premiere, but then, nobody else could get her to make public appearances. Many theaters across the country made bids for Grauman's Prologue. Sid refused, saying, "It would be impossible to transport the setting. We don't have to move the scenery in the Chinese, but to transport it elsewhere would wreck the entire structure. . . ." A complete model with a working elevator had been built on the stage to simulate the Grand Hotel lobby of the film. With John Barrymore, Joan Crawford, Garbo, Wallace Beery, and Lionel Barrymore in the best-selling novel of the times come to life on the screen, and their doubles in the Prologue, the Chinese Theater had another hit.

On July 5, 1932, Sid Grauman presented the world premiere of Eugene O'Neill's *Strange Interlude*, with Norma Shearer and Clark Gable. Sid's Prologue had an Olympic Games theme, to coincide with the international athletic event being held in Los Angeles that summer. Sid presented famous artists from all over the world, who had been brought to the theater expressly to contribute their talents to an ambitious stage presentation. Louella Parsons said of the Prologue: "Trust Sid to get in a timely note in his prologue. He gives a welcome to Olympic visitors in his stage setting, which represents the [Coliseum] stadium. His performers were brought here by Harry Weber and they furnish one of the best of the Grauman stage shows. . . . The Five Maxellos, equilibrists, and Lee and Shaw, comedians from the Phil Baker [radio] show, were well received. Likewise Gomez and Winona. Special dancers came from *Crazy Quilt* [the Broadway musical]. Particularly good is Frank Britton's band, direct from the Ziegfeld *Follies*. Sanami and Michl, weird Buddha dancers. The Joplin Kiddie dancers, and the Six Candreva Brothers, who play trumpets in harmony, complete a corking show. . . ." While the bill was still playing, Clarence "Buster" Crabbe won the 400-meter swimming final event and a gold medal. The Gumm Sisters (Judy Garland and her two siblings) were playing then at the Paramount, with Mrs. Gumm at the piano.

On September 9, 1932, Grauman presented a

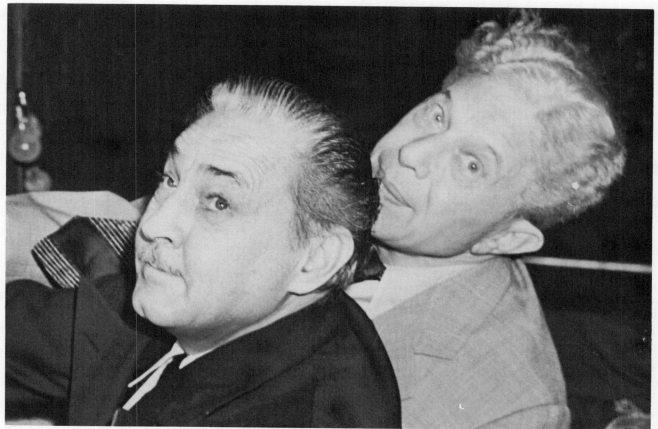

John Barrymore and Sid Grauman preparing for footprint ceremony in the Chinese Theater forecourt.

South Sea Prologue in conjunction with the world premiere of Joan Crawford in *Rain*. The opening night emcee was the ebullient comedian Eddie Cantor.

Sid reopened the United Artists Theater in downtown Los Angeles in October 1932, under the Skouras Brothers. Sid was also to supervise the Fox Pantages Theater in Hollywood. Both theaters would exhibit the same feature, the opener being MGM's *Red Dust* with Gable and Harlow. For stage fare, Grauman presented Fanchon and Marco's "Mystery" Revue at the United Artists and a capsule version of Ziegfeld's *Whoopee* with Buddy Doyle, staged by Leroy Prinz. Grauman was acting more and more in a purely executive capacity for stage show production and would never again reach the creative heights of his three important houses, the Million Dollar, the Egyptian, and the Chinese.

By November, Sid was listed as the general manager of all Fox West Coast Theaters in Los Angeles. Ads carried the banner "Under the direction of Sid Grauman." Undeniably, the Grauman name still

Tourists at Grauman's Chinese Theater viewing footprints of the stars in the theater's forecourt.

carried a good deal of commercial clout because in the past Sid had always given the public his complete entertainment deal.

The end of 1932 found the Chinese, Criterion, Million Dollar, Orpheum, and Carthay Circle theaters all closed. The new Los Angeles Theater, which had just opened in January 1931, was now also closed. The Depression was beginning to take its toll in the entertainment field.

From this time on, Sid was involved in Prologues only as a producer, not a creator. Many of his stage shows at various theaters were created by Fanchon and Marco, that indefatigable duo who were the busiest and most successful stage show entrepreneurs—after Sid Grauman—ever to present live productions in the Los Angeles area.

By 1933 times were getting even tougher for the Los Angeles theater scene. The United Artists closed once more, and Paramount Publix Theaters Corporation went bankrupt and into receivership. Paramount planned to sell most of its nationwide chain of houses. The downtown Paramount (formerly the Metropolitan) discontinued its stage shows in February 1933, reducing admission prices to twenty-five cents until 6:00 p.m., and forty cents until closing. Fox West Coast Theaters continued to present the Fanchon and Marco stage shows, but they had none of the opulence of the old Grauman shows. They were often presented with a band onstage, and featured singers and dancers against the house curtains. Loew's State and other comparable houses switched over to a pictures-only policy. Even the distinguished Chinese Theater was in trouble and Fox planned to close the house at the end of the run of Noel Coward's *Cavalcade* in February 1933.

In the same month the rising Japanese militarist bloc bombed cities in Asia, and the United States joined other nations in censuring Japan. Hitler's government was going to save the life of Germany as a nation, said Franz von Papen, and an old, exhausted von Hindenburg was forced to accept von Papen's word that Hitler could be held in check.

On March 3, 1933, President Franklin Roosevelt declared a Bank Holiday, and stores made every effort to assist patrons by accepting checks and giving change. Charge accounts were honored as usual. The Stock Exchange was closed, but Postal Savings was kept open. The Fox Theaters ran an ad in which they announced that "Checks Are Good. . . . Your personal check for the price of admission only during Bank Holiday at all Fox Theaters." Warner Brothers ran a similar advertisement.

On March 10, 1933, a heavy earthquake rocked the Los Angeles area. It was centered in Long Beach and caused widespread destruction. One hundred persons died and thousands were injured. Between the Bank Holiday and the quake disaster, theaters suffered a financial blow that was almost fatal for many of them. The city and county authorities in southern California kept people out of auditoriums and office buildings for a couple of weeks after the major quake, because of the unpredictability of aftershocks. In any event, due to the Bank Holiday most people had no money for entertainment.

When the Depression and subsequent events closed movie palaces all over the United States, the ambitious Fanchon and Marco team decided to take a bold step and try to revive business at some of the old movie palaces. They attempted this feat with the Roxy in New York and the Paramount in Los Angeles. They had more success on the West Coast than in the East.

The Los Angeles banks reopened in mid-March, with deposits leading withdrawals. Confidence in the economy seemed to be fully restored. The United States Senate voted $5 million for Los Angeles quake relief, while Mussolini was urging a five-year arms truce to maintain the peace in Europe.

During this time Sid Grauman was busy preparing for the premiere of *King Kong* at the Chinese Theater. Top prices were only $3.50 for the opening night. "Imagine attending a Chinese first night at this price!" an ad thrilled. *King Kong*, said Louella Parsons, ". . . is a Grauman opening in the full sense of the word. That master showman, Sid Grauman, who is full of original ideas, and good ones, outdoes himself. The prologue, appropriate to the picture with its voodoo dancers, rites to the sacred ape and eccentric dances of Zulus, puts one right into the mood for *King Kong*. African choral ensembles and choruses of dusky maidens were particularly good."

On May 25, 1933, publicity advised that Sid Grauman would have stage stars for his Prologue to *Gold Diggers of 1933*, Grauman would produce a miniature musical comedy onstage. Sid sent to New York for Albertina Rasch to stage the chorus ensemble, and Larry Ceballos directed. The show, called "Hollywood It Ain't" with a special musical score by Con Conrad, featured Jean Malin, Clarence Nordstrom, and Sam Ash, and was reviewed by Louella Parsons as "Distinct and different. . . . Sid is responsible for a take-off on the Brown Derby [Wilson Mizner's famous eatery]. . . . Auto-

Sid Grauman welcoming actor Barry Fitzgerald to Grauman's Chinese Theater in Hollywood in 1944.

Sid Grauman officiating at the signature ceremony for actress Frances Rafferty and comedian Red Skelton in the forecourt of Grauman's Chinese Theater (1942).

graph grabbers, dances, songs, in front and inside of the Brown Derby, got a big hand . . . [The Prologue] was so lengthy and has so many numbers that it is impossible to mention each one. . . . A medley of *Gold Diggers* song hits under the direction of Georgie Stoll completes the program. . . ."

Fated to become a film classic, the comedy *Dinner at Eight* came to the Chinese Theater in August 1933, with what was advertised as Sid Grauman's greatest Prologue, and certainly one of his most elaborate, featuring the Radio Rogues, the Sixteen Nifties, Ruth Harrison, Alex Fisher, Buck and Bubbles, the marvelous black dance team, and literally dozens of other features. The Los Angeles Grand Opera House setting in the late 1880s offered some excellent atmosphere. The film had a truly fabulous cast: Marie Dressler, Wallace Beery, Jean Harlow, Lionel Barrymore, Lee Tracy, Edmund Lowe, Billie Burke, Madge Evans, Jean Hersholt, Karen Morley, Phillips Holmes, and May Robson. It was directed by George Cukor.

Next was the world premiere of Mae West in *I'm No Angel*, featuring Cary Grant, with a Prologue called "Under the Big Top" on a reserved-seat, two-a-day basis. "The full blown charms of seductive Mae West were given the ultimate recognition in a Grauman Chinese premiere last night," said Louella Parsons. " 'Under the Big Top' reflected a gay carnival spirit. With a magnificent disregard for expense, Grauman imported the famous May Werth and her family of equestrians, Escolante, tightrope specialist, and other equally effective acts. . . . A highlight was Ray Huling and his trained seal, whose incredible antics kept the audience amazed and amused by turns."

Grauman was presenting Walter Winchell's *Broadway through a Keyhole* at the United Artists by November 1933, with humorist Chic Sale in a revue, a program similar to the early ones at the Million Dollar years before. On November 27, 1933, the Chinese Theater screened Eddie Cantor in *Roman Scandals*, and the Prologue was "Sidewalks of New York" in typical Grauman style. In December, Sid supervised another Chinese Theater show, *Little Women*, with Katharine Hepburn. Onstage was "A Christmas Prologue" with one hundred artists, set in a rural New England home. "Great entertainment for those who want to see a good show," said Louella Parsons.

On February 9, 1934, the fifty-fifth premiere was held at the Chinese Theater, to honor Greta

Sid Grauman officiating at the signature ceremony for
Anne Baxter and Gregory Peck in the forecourt of Grau-
man's Chinese Theater, December 1949. Four months later
Grauman was dead.

One of the mock ceremonies at the Breakfast Club. Sid Grauman is being awarded the "honorary" degree of Regular Fellow by fellow members. *Front row*: Joseph M. Schenck, Sid Grauman, Ruth Roland, and Dr. Rufus B. von Kleinsmid, president of U. S. C. *Back row*: Louis B. Mayer and Cecil B. De Mille.

Garbo (who still refused to make a public appearance to acknowledge Sid's courtesy). The film was the world premiere of MGM's *Queen Christina*, accompanied by Sid's "Regal Prologue" with a special overture by David Rose, and at purse-fitting prices. The Prologue featured prima ballerina Maria Gambarelli in "Moments from Grand Opera," and the entire Prologue was a court sequence laid in Queen Christina's palace.

In April 1934, Grauman's Chinese Theater witnessed a gala premiere for George Arliss in *The House of Rothschild*, with an effective Prologue. "Showman Sid Grauman . . . realized the perfect finale," said Louella Parsons. Thereafter the the-ater opened and closed with disconcerting irregularity, until a new policy was finally effected that eliminated the reserved seats and operated with a matinee and two evening performances daily on a general admission basis; four shows on Saturdays, Sundays, and holidays were regularly offered. Footlight entertainment, said the *Examiner*, would be of Grauman's customary originality and would accompany the presentations of first-class films. But the glory days for the Chinese Theater were over. Although the Chinese Theater would continue to remain a showplace until this era, the days of the grandiose Prologue were gone.

On October 17, 1934, rain spoiled an outdoor party for Sid Grauman given by the Hollywood Merchants' Association, who had planned to honor the impresario's anniversary as a theater exhibitor. The City Council nonetheless adopted a resolution to thank Grauman for the great service he had rendered in building up "our most distinctive Industry" and congratulating him upon the anniversary.

The days of the great Prologues were finished as a regular Los Angeles feature by 1935. Although stage shows continued at the Chinese Theater for some time, the excitement of those early extravaganzas would never be restored to the stage either at the Chinese or in any other Los Angeles house. Some fine shows were presented in conjunction with films, but as films became more able to supplant the live shows to the customers' complete satisfaction, stage entertainment was diminished in scope, until it finally ceased altogether. Mounting costs plus public indifference sounded the death knell to the Prologue as conceived and perpetuated from the Million Dollar's prime in 1918 through the advent of sound pictures into the mid-1930s.

Sid Grauman continued to have a hand in various productions around the Los Angeles area for many years, but by 1938 the Graumanesque Prologue was a dead dinosaur. In June 1942, an advertisement announced the opening of the El Capitan Theater on Vine Street with *The Blackouts of 1942*, starring Ken Murray, Billy Gilbert, Marie Wilson, the Nicholas Brothers, Gene Austin, Betty Atkinson, Park and Clifford, Roy Daley, and others. The theater was under the management of Matt Allen and Sid Grauman. Florence Lawrence said of the show: "Whenever there was or was not a pause of any kind, Murray or Gilbert, or both, were right there putting a little added tempo and plenty of laughs into the production which is scheduled for a run at the beautifully decorated theater. . . ." Schallert said that Ken Murray and Billy Gilbert, as impresarios, and Allen and Grauman as sponsors, had a very good show. "It is blithesomely contrived and drew an audience [that was] warmly responsive to the premiere. Mae West was in the theater, as well as Al Jolson, Rudy Vallee and others prominent in the entertainment sphere. . . . Murray called on Grauman from the audience to take a bow at the close. . . ."

The Blackouts, in various forms, ran for years and was the last successful association of Sid Grauman with Los Angeles theaters. Sid made occasional public appearances from time to time, but his failing health, as much as any other factor, removed him from the active Los Angeles theatrical scene. His absence was missed and mourned by many.

13

AT the October 27, 1949, Hollywood Chamber of Commerce testimonial banquet honoring Sid Grauman, the publicity director of the Roosevelt Hotel, Brigg Townsend, spoke warmly of his years as Grauman's press agent to the *Citizen News*:

Sid received dozens of requests all the time for financial aid. And he came through generously for every worthwhile case. He used to ask me, "Do I know this person?" in referring to a letter asking for aid, and if I was able to identify the person and he deserved help, Sid would oblige. Many was the time I heard him say, "Send this old friend of mine $200." Grauman, you see, had suffered pangs of hunger in his early [Alaska] days trying to get a foothold on Life's ladder, and he never forgot what it was like. He is still helping people all the time—those who deserve it—but you never hear about it. He is very shy about having it known.

Leaders from all walks of life turned out for the gala celebration to honor Sid Grauman. Los Angeles Mayor Fletcher Bowren was there, and California Governor Earl Warren, Los Angeles Sheriff Biscailuz, and Judge Harlan G. Palmer, made rare personal appearances to pay homage to Sid.

Mayor Bowren remarked with wry good humor that Sid might just be "one of the *few* good things to come to us from San Francisco." Sheriff Biscailuz recalled his first meeting with Grauman in San Francisco in 1912. Judge Palmer noted that the mayor had spoken for many thousands who admired Sid, and Sheriff Biscailuz had spoken for the pioneers. "So I shall speak for myself," he said, turning to Grauman. "I salute you for your substantial contributions to Hollywood and the entertainment world at large."

Actor Frank Fay took over as toastmaster and began to introduce an impressive list of notables: Joseph Schenck, Darryl Zanuck, Jack L. Warner, Jean Hersholt, Edward Arnold, Jesse Lasky, Mack Sennett, Jack Benny, Leo Carillo, and Attorney Joseph Scott. Female stars attending included Jeanette MacDonald, Marie Wilson, Barbara Britton, Ginger Rogers, and Linda Darnell. Dewy-eyed Ginger Rogers showed her affection for Sid by kissing him on the cheek. Sophie Tucker told how Sid had wooed her away from a theater across the street from Grauman's Empress in San Francisco by offering her considerably more money than she was already making. "I accepted," Tucker said, "and when I reported for work, there was Sid himself putting my name up on the marquee."

When Grauman was finally introduced to the banquet assemblage around midnight, the applause was warm and prolonged. Starting to express his gratitude for the occasion, Sid was suddenly overcome with tears at the admiration and well-wishing of those present. But, trouper that he was, Sid recovered control quickly. After dwelling briefly on the value of friendship he recounted some of his early experiences. He told how he and his father David got started in show business in Dawson, Alaska, and of his early training in his father's troupe of Georgia Minstrels, his exhibitor's career in San Francisco, his legitimate road show productions at various times in his life, and his eventual permanent residence in Los Angeles and the founding of his several Los Angeles theaters. Sid concluded his short speech with many thanks to all his friends for the kind words of affection, modestly overlooking the fact that his truly unique talent for friendship, as well as his theatrical achievements, had made the testimonial banquet the highly emotional moment that it was.

Some eighteen years earlier, Louella O. Parsons's daughter Harriet had written a *Keyhole Portrait of Sid* in the *Examiner* of January 3, 1932. In its chatty way the piece gives a vivid glimpse of Grauman:

Sid has two vices besides practical jokes. One is his passion for Oriental objects which sparked the design of the Chinese. He spends preposterous sums on Chinese curios . . . preferably large ones . . . and gives them to his friends. . . . He likes plaid suits . . . and has the loudest pair of bathing trunks on the West Coast. . . . He's an ardent practicing Christian Scientist. . . . He loves to visit the sick. . . . His mother's name is Rosa. Like her son, she is one of the film colony's most interesting figures, an accomplished pianist and composer . . . and Sid's devotion to her is historical in Hollywood. . . . Sid is a good and loyal friend, well-liked by local merchants and businessmen. His shock of wiry hair is amazing; when he wore it in a long bob [the first Afro] he caused heads to turn. When he cut it, it marked the passing of an era, and Hollywood lost its most famous landmark. . . . Sid doesn't smoke or drink. . . .

On February 14, 1932, Marquis Busby wrote in the *Examiner* about film-city laughmakers and their practical jokes that won big hands. Though he cited "the gentle humor of playwright Frederick Lonsdale, the polite witticisms of Philip Barry, the irony of Noel Coward" as snicker-provoking, he emphasized that practical jokes of a rudimentary sort were the big roar in Hollywood. "Such stories race all over town," said Busby.

There are shrieks at the Brown Derby, at Sardi's, at the Vendome, and each person who tells the joke adds his own embellishment. Before the day is out the joke has been accredited to everyone from Jackie Cooper to Charlie Chaplin.

The genial impresario of the Chinese was known to sit up nights working out new jokes to spring on friends. One time the plotting Sid stretched himself out in bed in his hotel room after applying a liberal dose of death pallor make-up and sprinkling a bottle of catsup judiciously about. Then he had an accomplice summon his physician post haste. [His doctor was Harry Martin, the husband of Louella O. Parsons.] Martin was given quite a start, for he knew that Sid had recently lost a lot on the stock market—until, of course, Sid sat up and grinned at him.

In her loving tribute to Grauman just a few days before his death, Louella Parsons gave a different version of the incident:

There are hundreds of stories about Grauman's jokes, but one that I happen to know very well, since it concerns my husband, Dr. Harry Martin, is the time that Sid was supposed to be in New York.

Faking a long distance call from the East, Sid asked the doctor to go to his suite in the Los Angeles Ambassador Hotel and get his studs and tuxedo and send them to him in New York. It was during the stock market crash, and Sid had lost considerable money and was very depressed.

Dr. Martin had to go through a lot of red tape to get into the hotel room. When he finally walked in, there was Sid lying apparently dead on the floor—ticker tape all over him and what looked like blood, but it was really only ketchsup [sic], all over his face.

The bellboy ran screaming from the room, and the manager almost fainted. Finally the "dead" man got up, yawned, and greeted everyone!

Another variation of this gag has Sid summoning Charlie Chaplin to his room with a frantic phone call to view the bloody corpse of a woman whom Sid confessed to having killed. Charlie became so hysterical that finally Sid had to lead him over to the dummy "corpse" to convince him that the whole thing was a put-on, after which Charlie was more upset than ever.

Anyone who knew Sid at all knew that he was a great teller of jokes. Stories of Sid's jokes were still circulating around Hollywood long after his death.

Once Sid and Joseph Schenck decided to liven up Sid's place of residence (the Alexandria Hotel) where Sid lived for many years, a favorite pleasuring point for actors in the wild 1920s. The two men dressed in workmen's coveralls and caps and removed the rug from the hotel lobby.

Another time Sid told theater owner Tom Tally that a group of visiting exhibitors wanted Tally to speak to them about his expertise in theater operation. Sid led Tully into a dimly lighted room with rows of chairs occupied by a strangely silent audience. Tally was well into a fiery speech on the methods of film exhibiting before he caught on to the fact that his audience was composed of studio dummies, all set up by Sid.

When Grauman wasn't pulling stunts with Schenck, he was doing them with William S. Hart, a favorite early fellow prankster. Adolph Zukor at the age of eighty told of a trip that he made by train from New York to Los Angeles. At a stop not far out of Los Angeles, two men dressed as cowboys with bandana kerchiefs tied across their noses walked into the Pullman car where Zukor had a compartment and shoved six-shooters into the producer's face, demanding his valuables.

The terrified passengers on the train scuttled into hiding, but Zukor glanced mildly at the steely eyes of the taller of the two bandits. He had seen that same gaze often enough in Hart's films. He also noted the frizzy hair straying from beneath the ten-gallon hat worn by the shorter bandit.

"Hello there, Bill," he murmured. "Hello, Sid."

Zukor spent a portion of his eightieth birthday placing his prints in the Chinese Theater forecourt. Asked why he had not done it sooner when Sid Grauman was alive, Zukor smiled and said, "Confidentially, I was afraid to do it then. Sid would have found some way to get me stuck down there for good!"

William S. Hart figured in another of Sid's stunts that failed to ignite. As a joke on his patrons, Sid conceived the idea of having Lon Chaney put on Oriental makeup and act as the head usher for one performance at the Chinese Theater. Hart had given Lon Chaney his first big chance in films, and the Man of a Thousand Faces, as Chaney was called, agreed to the gag out of friendship for Hart. But before the hoax could be pulled off, Louis B. Mayer somehow got wind of it. Mayer took a very dim view of his popular character star publicizing anything that wasn't MGM property, so he hurried

down to the Chinese Theater and told all three men where they could go and guaranteed to help them get there if he ever heard of such shenanigans again.

Harriet Parsons also had a story about Sid's pranks:

[His] jokes are as spectacular as his prologues. . . . There's no limit to the time, money and energy he'll spend to put over a "rib". . . . But his laugh is not so hearty when the tables are turned on him. . . . It happens occasionally. . . . For instance, the time he sent a live goose to Doug and Mary. . . . He had it placed in the drawing room of their private railroad car and eagerly awaited reports of their embarrassment [they were en route by train to New York]. . . . But Doug and Mary went along with the gag, and calmly had the goose served up as a dinner dish. . . . Sid wept when he heard about it. . . . You see, it was a trained goose . . . and its weekly salary was $750. . . . It cost Sid quite a lot to placate the owner. . . .

Sid topped most of his other practical jokes when the Warner brothers were laying the cornerstone to their Hollywood Boulevard theater. Stars, civic luminaries, and film notables of every magnitude appeared at the ceremony. Celebrities arrived in lavish limousines to the ecstatic oohs and ahs of a vast army of fans in the bleachers. As an interested rival, with his Egyptian and Chinese houses operating successfully, Sid Grauman also attended. But he hired a hearse, complete with pallbearers, and drove up to the klieg-lighted arrival pad. In a coffin Sid was carried solemnly to the cornerstone. The coffin lid was opened and Sid sat up, climbed out, and shook hands with the Warners. The brothers were hopping mad at him for quite a while but ultimately forgave him. Very few people could stay mad at Sid long for his pranks.

Once in 1929, a joke of another sort was played on Sid. He had a rule when he lived at the Ambassador Hotel that he was not to be disturbed before noon, since he usually went to work at his theaters around 7:00 p.m. and continued to work until dawn. When the stock market crashed, Sid could probably have salvaged some of his considerable wealth. Instead he took a terrible beating because no calls from his broker got through to him. It was reputed that he was worth more than $6 million at the time, but the crash wiped him out. Sid didn't even whimper, so sources say. His motto always was, "Chalk it up to experience," when things went wrong. And he must have applied that philosophy then. He never failed to learn from doing.

Grauman had very few close relatives, although thirteen people put in claims on his estate. (He left no will.) At the news of his death, telegrams arrived from all over the country from people who claimed kinship to the showman, or demanded a share in his estate for other reasons. On April 22, 1950, a few weeks after Sid's death, a Mrs. Carrie Adair, forty-eight, made the claim that Grauman had picked her up as a lonely fourteen-year-old in the El Paso, Texas, railway station thirty-four years earlier and that she lived with the impresario for four years.

The testimony was offered by Mrs. Adair at a deposition hearing before Attorney Frank Gunter who represented four of Grauman's cousins who were making claim to a share in the $750,000 estate left by Grauman. Mrs. Adair sought $32,000 on grounds that a crudely printed "will" (shades of the Howard Hughes incident) had left her that amount. Mrs. Adair said that she had run away from her San Antonio home in 1916 and was alone in the El Paso depot when Grauman chanced upon her and suggested an alliance.

"Come along with me," she said he told her, "and I'll get you a job."

Mrs. Adair claimed that she lived with Grauman for over four years in two different downtown Los Angeles hotels, and that Grauman spent every night with her.

"We were just as good as married, he said when I asked him to marry me," stated Mrs. Adair.

During the deposition, the claimant showed a scar on her arm which she swore was made by Grauman's teeth. "I always mark my women" was Grauman's declaration, according to the claimant. "Every man should leave his brand on his women."

At the time of the alleged meeting, Grauman was thirty-six and a successful theater operator in northern California. The judge refused to hear the case and threw it out of court.

On the day of Sid's funeral at Forest Lawn, Matt Weinstock said in the *Daily News* that all the eulogies

pointed up his great showmanship as exemplified by the rococo Chinese Theater, with its footprints of stars in the forecourt cement. The Chinese may have been his triumph, but to those who go back that far, his greatest achievement will always be The Million Dollar, his pioneer effort. . . . In this equally rococo structure, he achieved the setting that became the nation's pattern for motion picture entertainment [for a whole generation]. Those who were around will probably never forget the organ interludes. Between the newsreel and the feature, the theater would be darkened and changing colored spotlights would be played on a tiny figure in the vast amphitheater seated at the console down in the pit. . . . Jesse Crawford or Henry Murtagh, playing wonderfully soothing melodies. The experience was the nearest many people ever got to church.

Sid Grauman's remarkable ability to move his audiences, to take a mere wisp of an idea and clothe it skillfully with undeniable elegance, even that organ interlude, was partly responsible for the distinguished career he made of everything he touched. But the balance of his success must be attributed to his fine personality and to his strong character, both of which were colored by his great talent for friendship. Affable, considerate, generous, shrewd, and ingenious, a warm friend or business associate, Sid Grauman was also a visionary who knew instinctively how to materialize his dreams and reach the general public with them.

Sid Grauman died on March 5, 1950, less than two weeks short of his seventy-first birthday. Very few who knew his life and work would deny that he had a true touch of genius with Prologues and people.

Appendix 1
About the Prologues

Don Samson wrote in the *Exhibitors Herald/Moving Picture World* of January 18, 1930, that theaters in the very near future might return to the prologue form of stage show entertainment that they had quickly abandoned the moment film began to speak. "This," said Samson, "was brought about mainly by the recent success of many pictures when presented with an appropriate stage show. A stage show that coincided with a feature picture 'creates' an atmosphere that helps considerably to present the picture in a more colorful manner. Theater managers are beginning to realize that any picture, regardless of quality, needs something more than itself to stimulate the box office."

The Roxy Theater in New York was supplementing the film *Hot for Paris* with a light, colorful stage program that carried the theme of the picture. Other key movie houses in several big cities across the country were following suit.

"I believe," Samson continued,

> that the first man to really attract attention by presenting elaborate prologues with his pictures was Sid Grauman in his Hollywood Egyptian Theater. Today one could easily say that he is more famous for his colorful prologues than any other achievement. He was a real showman who could look ahead and see its [the Prologue's] possibilities. For several years the drawing power of his theater was built around this flesh form of entertainment.
>
> There is something consistent in a program carried out in this style. . . . Besides the entertainment value in itself, it goes a long way toward putting the audience in the proper mood for the feature picture. This was the real reason why the prologue form of entertainment was originated. . . . There is no dispute that theater audiences like the times are changing, but the present state of flesh entertainment is without a doubt due only to those in charge of it. . . . The stage show field has unlimited possibilities . . . [with] a scope that could not be covered in the next hundred years, but only because of the strides the motion picture has made in the last couple of years, the producer as well as the talent of the stage presentation have become discouraged. If the stage show or any other form of flesh entertainment ever becomes passe, it will only be the fault of poor showmanship. I overheard just the other day a famous vaudeville artist say, "Our stuff is out now; what's the use of trying? All we can do is go on until we're forced out altogether." It is this spirit that is hurting more than anything else.

Samson's crusading optimism was admirable, but his hopes for a renaissance of the Prologue were to prove pretty much in vain. The appearance of stars at premieres still occurs as an adjunct to the film presentation, but there are, unfortunately, no Prologues, and a rigid separateness stands between the legitimate stage show and the motion picture.*

Since the Prologue as Grauman created it is a lost art, or at best a defunct one, it might be interesting to take a look at some aspects of the show that made Sid Grauman world-famous and see what actually happened behind the footlights.

The Grauman Prologues generally followed an orchestral overture and some short subjects to warm up the audience. The Prologues were presented before the half-time intermission and preceding the feature film, and were usually related to the picture. Terry Helgesen wrote in his *Console* magazine brochure on the Chinese Theater on January 18, 1932. For this film, Grauman presented Lottie Mayer's Diving Ballet in an unsurpassed spectacle. Seventy-five girls dressed in Louis XVI costumes and wigs pranced down several stairways and into a central reflecting pool in the stage floor, disappearing beneath the water (and coming up somewhere backstage, of course). Out of sight the pearing beneath the water (and coming up somewhere backstage, of course). Out of sight the girls zipped into pearl-studded leotards and shell headdresses through which sprays of water could be ejected. Then they marched back up through the pool and onto the stairways, which were equipped with twenty-one fountains at various levels. The fountains and the spraying headdresses were cross-lit with multicolored spotlights so that the whole stage coruscated with prismatic light and seemed to be a living rainbow of a million flashing colored jewels. At stage level in front of the showgirls were ballet girls, each waving pairs of enormous ostrich-feather fans, white on one side and rainbow-hued on the other. It was quite a sight, Helgesen wrote, and undoubtedly brought audiences to the theater who were not necessarily Garbo fans.

For the film *Broadway Melody*, Grauman augmented a marvelous singing and dancing Prologue with 150 Albertina Rasch Ballet girls. The finale took place on a stairway that was the width of the stage and the height of the proscenium. The entire cast paraded down the stairway, disappeared into the wings, and then raced backstage to the

*The Chinese Theater premiered *Grease* on June 6, 1978, with John Travolta, Olivia Newton-John, Alice Cooper, and Andy Gibb among the stars present.

ramp again and repeated this descent in a continuous line. From the audience it seemed that a cast of endless thousands of artists had been hired. At the conclusion of the parade, all the costumes reversed into a huge flower garden that filled the entire stage with a riot of color.

Grauman's ideas, says Helgesen, were basically quite simple in their concept, and nearly always spectacular. Sid would take an elementary idea, as he did in *The Covered Wagon* at the Egyptian—turning small wagons into larger ones—and build a whole theme show around it. The idea of the flower garden was borrowed from the *Broadway Melody* Prologue by Fanchon and Marco, who staged many Grauman shows, when they presented the premiere stage show that opened the beautiful Fox Theater in San Francisco in 1929.

With Joan Crawford's *Rain* at the Chinese Theater, the last act of the Prologue was a famous acrobatic and adagio team, performing in a San Francisco Chinatown set. Their act was climaxed when the man swung his partner by her hair and finally tossed her through a fake plate-glass window, bringing the police, sirens, and so on. At that point the set split and revolved to become the movie set of a seedy tropical hotel. Palm trees slid in from either wing, and tropical foliage was lowered from the flies, all duplicating the film's main set. Doubles of Crawford and principal cast members sauntered out onto the hotel veranda and the rain began to descend in torrents, as the golden curtains slowly closed, bringing the intermission before the film and vividly setting the atmosphere for the film to come.

Young readers may wonder about the large casts that Grauman assembled for his Prologues, and how he could do this and still make a profit. The enormous casts were not simply advertising hyperbole—Grauman actually did use the numbers of people he claimed. But he did, however, employ extras, the same as those who were being used in motion pictures. In the early days of the Million Dollar and the Egyptian theaters, these extras were paid a dollar a performance. In the late days of the Chinese Theater, this sum was increased. Crowds of actors would gather at the stage door of the Egyptian and the Chinese theaters before each matinee and evening performance. A stage manager would hire the people he needed according to the size and shape that would fit the costumes he had to fill. After they were picked, the actors were given their costumes by wardrobe and were instructed where and when they were to appear on the stage. They were guided through actual performances by the regulars.

If this now seems like a strange procedure in today's show business world of rigid unions, it worked out very well for Grauman and other exhibitors and allowed the Prologues to be opulently populated with scores of participants, who often numbered as high as 200. The regular dancers, singers, and specialty acts were all properly rehearsed and worked under run-of-the-show contracts.

If Grauman found an act he considered to be exceptional, he would present it in front of his famous ermine curtain, an incredible showpiece made of white brushed velvet and hung with ermine-dyed foxtails. Helgesen says that this curtain was also used as a background when stars were introduced at the various premieres.

Sid's Chinese Theater Prologues were presented, off and on, for about a decade. In the later years, Fanchon and Marco presented the Prologues for Sid. The Grauman name remained on the Chinese Theater for many years, for which Sid was paid a fee. With the premiere of *Windjammer* the theater was renovated and the Grauman name was removed.

"Small wonder," Florence Lawrence said in a 1927 piece on Grauman,

> that Grauman prologues entrance the world. Sid weaves the spell of his prologues like an olden magician. They are conceived in happiness, developed in good will. Mr. Grauman, adept at whatever has to do with the theater, is like some master magician of old. But he searches no hoary parchment for his inspiration, he invokes no mystic aids to his incantations. Rather he works in sunlight. Gay California breezes filter through orange curtains at his windows; the splash of falling water murmurs from the Chinese forecourt fountain beneath his window. Soft strains of music and the kaleidoscope of gorgeous fabrics from which he chooses his next prologue's costumes sets his mind atune to the business of entertainment.
> Grauman is never so thoroughly content with his work as when creating a new stage effect for a picture. He still speaks with tenderness of his current picture, *King of Kings*. In this film he feels that De Mille and the Chinese have brought a great boon to Los Angeles. In the first four months of show, this sacred drama with its marvelous prologue has attracted more than

500,000 spectators, many of them, said Grauman, were making their first visit inside the walls of a theater to see the life [and face] of Christ revealed for the first time in a major presentation. [The Pilgrimage Play in the Hollywood Hills opposite the Hollywood Bowl represented Christ as a visible figure, but no important film had ever shown Jesus full-face before.] Grauman calls the silversheet a great medium for public inspiration and education. . . .

In future showings, *King of Kings* never achieved quite the religious impact that it had at the Chinese Theater, largely a result of the stunning effect of Grauman's spectacularly colorful though deeply reverent Prologue.

One of the reasons that Sid Grauman's Prologues moved across the stage of the Chinese Theater with such amazing precision was the use of the latest technology behind the scenes. Grauman searched constantly for new aids to simplify theater administration. No innovation was too advanced or unusual for Sid to consider.

In an interview with *Motion Picture News*, published on February 4, 1928, Sid discussed the problem of management in a theater as large as the Chinese and explained how he coped with it.

> The most urgent problem in theater management is, of course, a perfect performance [said Sid]. All units contributing to the audience's entertainment must operate with clocklike precision. There must be no breaks in the program.
> There are several methods of synchronizing these various units . . . to assure a smooth performance. . . . The most efficient is . . . the Dictograph, an interior telephone system for the house.
> The Dictograph Corporation had several of its engineers spend a good part of a year studying theater communication problems. . . . I had the pleasure of being a consultant, and several of my suggestions are now a standard feature of the Theater Dictograph.

At that moment in the interview there was a soft click, not much louder than a pencil tap— the stage manager calling Sid on the Dictograph. Sid depressed a key on the walnut-finished cabinet and was conversing easily with the staff member about a change in the operating schedule. Returning moments later to the interview, Sid continued, "This little cabinet with its twenty keys gives me immediate access to any part of the theater, telling me who's calling even before I answer. It leaves a memo of calls which come in while I'm out. It gives me preferential calls throughout the system by a special right-of-way circuit which precludes the possibility of a busy line, a feature exclusive with Dictograph. . . I should like to have Mr. Reed, the manager, take you round [the theater]. . . ."

Whereupon Sid threw five keys, and when all parties came on the line, he said that he was sending round the interviewer, Carl J. Begemann, with Reed. "Please extend all courtesies," Grauman requested. In one operation he had accomplished what would have taken ten minutes and five calls with a regular phone. Sid took Begemann to meet Reed in his office.

Manager Reed pointed out the master station on his desk. "Identical to Mr. Grauman's control," he said, "except that it connects to different points. This key is wired to a bank of microphones in the footlights, so whenever I want to monitor the progress of the stage show, I throw this key and the loudspeaker brings in music, dialogue, dancers' shuffling feet, noisy scene shifting—every sound onstage. . . And *this* key is wired to a microphone in the lobby's wall paneling. I can hear what patrons say about the show as they leave, which often brings us valuable information about the program. Sometimes we even make changes, based on the comment we get."

In the projection room Reed pointed out that a small Dictograph substation was installed on each side of the four picture projectors. These instruments were wired in multiple so that incoming calls could be received without the operator having to change his position.

Attached to the orchestra podium was a small Dictograph substation. Reed explained that sometimes an emergency call must be made from backstage to the podium, or from the projection room to the podium. "To gain time for projection difficulties or for scene shifting, etc., the stage manager may have to request an extended musical interlude. This has proven a distinct advance over the light signal," Reed said, pointing to a red button light next to a white one that lit up whenever a call was made.

At the organ console, the organist was already tuning up the instrument for the matinee performance. He ran his hands skillfully over the keyboards. Noticing an off-pitch sound, he waited un-

til the acoustic vibration subsided, and then pressed a key on his Dictograph substation attached to the console.

"Please make number 8A a bit finer," the organist requested into his microphone, and in a minute there was a buzz on the instrument from the tuner up in the overhead organ loft with instructions to try that same key again.

The organist explained that the organ chamber interior was huge; it ran from the floor right up and into the ceiling. The adjusting had to be done on several floor levels. The sound made by one of the pipes reached such volume in the loft that the tuner could not hear the result of his adjustment. In houses without the Dictograph, the tuner must emerge from the loft to hear. But the Dictograph provided six locations throughout the organ loft for six phone jacks wired to the console. The tuner was equipped with a headset and breast transmitter attached to a long cord that terminated in a plug. By inserting the jack in the nearest outlet, the organist was automatically buzzed, and then by lifting his receiver, the organist and tuner were connected by regular phone contact. And when the organist signaled the tuner, a light appeared simultaneously on all six floor levels, where it was visible from any position in the chamber.

In the main lobby Reed pointed out a flush type of Dictograph used to communicate with the head usher.

"Our policy," Reed said, "is not to sell more tickets than seats. From this station the head usher calls the box office and can keep up-to-the-minute on ticket sales and match that with seat availability."

The Dictograph was an innovative system, which was probably a delight for Grauman who liked gadgets that were also practical. The system was applied to large and small theaters eventually with varying adaptations. Always keen on any aid that would work toward achieving flawless operation and better performances, Sid was among the first of the theater impresarios to apply the new system to a house as massive as the Chinese. Considering that the year was 1928, Grauman foresaw the advantages of instant electronic communication aids some decades before they became standard operating equipment everywhere.

Appendix 2
The Grauman Honors

On the night of January 11, 1927, a varied mix of thirty-six film notables gathered together by mutual interest for dinner at the Ambassador Hotel in Los Angeles. They were assembled to discuss the formation of a body to celebrate, solemnize, and promote the motion picture industry. All present felt that it was about time the filmmakers blew their own horn and had a definitive hand in the worldwide acknowledgment of quality film production.

Among the many distinguished persons present, according to Richard Shale's *Academy Awards* Frederick Ungar Reference Index, were J. Arthur Ball, pioneer film engineer; Richard Barthelmess, actor; Cecil B. De Mille, director; Douglas Fairbanks, Sr., actor; Cedric Gibbons, art director; Benjamin Glazer, writer; Sid Grauman, veteran movie exhibitor; Jack Holt, actor; Henry King, director; Frank Lloyd, director; Harold Lloyd, actor-producer; Jeanie McPherson, writer; Louis B. Mayer, producer; Bess Meredyth, writer; Conrad Nagel, actor; Fred Niblo, director; Mary Pickford, actress; Harry Rapf, producer; Joseph M. Schenck, producer; Milton Sills, actor; John Stahl, director; Irving G. Thalberg, producer; Raoul Walsh, director; Harry Warner, producer; and Carey Wilson, writer.

The Academy of Motion Picture Arts and Sciences was created as the result of that Ambassador Hotel dinner. Founded fifty-five years ago by this group, the Academy contained personnel who represented various branches of the industry, and through the decades it has accrued increasing fame and varying measures of respect for its annual awards and television coverage.

Sometimes it takes the Academy an unconscionably long period to recognize the contributions of various artists, but ultimately just dues are paid to outstanding film industry talents. In 1948 the Academy awarded a special statuette to Sid Grauman. At the presentation ceremony Sid was lauded as a "master showman who raised the standard of motion picture exhibition to a high art" and was commended for his achievement. "Several decades of artists and movie-goers owe a great deal to the glamour that Sid Grauman brought to his profession of motion picture impresario."

The Academy that Sid helped to found had waited a long time to give official recognition of what was common knowledge among the vast army of Los Angeles theater patrons who had been dazzled by Sid's spectacular presentations from 1918 through 1928, and intermittently thereafter. The Academy's statuette award to Sid Grauman came two years before his death and was an appropriate climax to a career that truly began in the Yukon and ended in Hollywood, where Sid had no betters in his field.

Appendix 3
A Talk with Stewart Brady

Stewart Brady, singer, pianist, and voice teacher, lives in a handsome old house on Jackson Street in San Francisco only a short distance from the Pacific Heights entrance to the Presidio. The vocal coach for San Francisco's prestigious American Conservatory Theater, Stewart works at home among treasured souvenirs of the musical past, but he is very much a man of the present who enjoys talking about his life and work.

Born in June 1916, Stewart began his musical career as a small child, evincing exceptional talent from the time he was nine months old. His parents were Nevadans who used their musical ability to form a vaudeville act that played for years on the Orpheum circuit along with such headliners as the durable Sophie Tucker. Mr. Brady played violin and trumpet, Mrs. Brady sang and danced.

Stewart came to the attention of theatrical impresario Gus Edwards when the latter attended a musicale at San Francisco's Fairmont Hotel that featured the ten-year-old Stewart. Gus Edwards was perhaps the outstanding discoverer and promoter of juvenile talent in his day. His subsequent mention of Stewart's ability to Sid Grauman in Los Angeles piqued Sid's interest. Eventually Stewart went south to audition for Grauman while the *King of Kings* Prologue was in rehearsal at the Chinese Theater.

Of this audition Stewart says that Sid Grauman asked him if he had any religious music he particularly liked. Stewart recalls,

To this question my mother nearly fell over. She knew exactly what I was going to say, because I was very fond of the Negro spiritual, *Were You There When They Crucified My Lord*? So before all the cast in their costumes---they'd been rehearsing for hours---I said to Mr. Grauman, "Yes, I have." So I sang it for him.

When I'd finished, Mr. Grauman said, "Stewart, I'm afraid it'll be too much. I don't think people could take it. Do you have anything that's bright and cheery?"

And I said, "How about *The Holy City*?"

He said, "Great! Do you know it?"

And I said no, but that I'd have it for him by tomorrow. So we went out and got the sheet music, I learned and sang it for him the next day and he said, "That's it!"---and I was hired.

Stewart further recalls, "At the time I sang *The Holy City* there was a full orchestra accompanying me. Vladimir Bakaleinikoff was our conductor. Now I didn't like Vladimir because he was always throwing things in without telling me. Once I was standing in the wings complaining about the conductor when a large man approached me and asked if I would like him to take over. I was delighted and said yes. It was Constantin Bakaleinikoff, Vladimir's brother. He conducted and there was no more trouble."

Stewart tells of the illustrious opening night of *King of Kings*, one of the most awesome and glamorous in Hollywood history. "There was such an ovation for my closing Prologue number that although the picture had started, Mr. Grauman stopped it and said to me, 'I promise never to ask you again, but will you sing *The Holy City* once more?' So I sang another chorus and the film began again."

Grauman was such a perfectionist, Stewart recalls, that even on the day of the premiere the Prologue cast rehearsed in costume until it was almost showtime. Stewart says he can never remember being so exhausted. Food was brought in, however, since Grauman was always considerate of his cast and staff. "Being in that production was one of the most marvelous experiences of my life and the memory of it affects me strongly," Stewart says emotionally. "Sid Grauman was never fully appreciated in the proper way. There were a lot of crass and insensitive people around Hollywood in those days who didn't understand his talent. He was also a great gentleman, a kindly man. Many weren't able to give him the recognition he deserved for his brilliant work. Quiet and soft-spoken, he still knew exactly what he wanted and how to get this from his people at all times. That is talent."

Stewart states, "When I left *King of Kings* Mr. Grauman gave me his father's watch. He said I had given the finest consecutive performances in his theater and he wanted me to have David J. Grauman's watch. It was an old Hamilton with a crystal face that screwed off, and I still have it. Characteristically, the thought was the important gesture, for he had wrapped the precious gift in old newspaper before he presented it to me."

Sid's mother, Rosa, was a fine pianist who was already quite aged at the time the Chinese Theater opened. Once Sid brought his mother to the theater and had her lowered into the orchestra pit to play Bach, Chopin, and many other composers as Sid sat in an orchestra seat listening to her.

"She was excellent," Stewart points out, and no one was happier over her unusual concert than Grauman himself.

Stewart says that he joined rehearsals for the *King of Kings* Prologue when they were already in progress for some time. It was three more weeks of grueling preparation before the Prologue was presented. Even though he was a child, Stewart was required by Sid Grauman to attend all rehearsals. An insomniac, Sid would sometimes phone Stewart and get him out of bed in the middle of the night with suggestions for changes in the Prologue until finally the showman realized that he was dealing with a young boy who needed his rest, and he stopped the practice.

Although Stewart left the *King of Kings* company, Grauman called the singer often after the show's six-month run through November 3, 1927. Stewart returned to the stage of the Chinese Theater a year later on November 1, 1928, to sing in the Prologue of *Noah's Ark*, another biblical epic. After that, Sid continued to call Stewart from time to time to ask him how things were going. Stewart says he saw Grauman only once after the run of *Noah's Ark*, and that was on the street in San Francisco.

As was done in earlier days, Stewart was under formal contract simultaneously to Grauman, Fox Studios, and Warner Brothers. He made four film short subjects during this time, but he didn't like Hollywood and felt very strongly even at that early age that he was wasting his musical ability by staying on. So he asked Grauman to release him from his theater contract. Sid did so graciously, saying, "Aren't you fortunate to find out what you want at your age?"

Stewart not only came by his teaching and singing talents naturally, he made use of his talents from the beginning of his Grauman days. "The first lesson I ever gave was to a lovely young Mexican girl named Helene Apel in the *King of Kings* Prologue chorus. She had a gorgeous contralto, a tiny little thing, fabulously talented. I coached her and others heard about it. They came in droves, and there I was, suddenly a boy voice teacher. Grauman was pleased."

Modest about his superb boy's soprano, Stewart went on to become a pupil of the illustrious Italian tenor, Dino Borgioloi, and eventually studied with him in Italy.

"I performed my first arpeggio when I was nine

months old, following my mother while she sang," he explains. Singing, however, is not Stewart's greatest love, and he no longer sings professionally. What he enjoys most is teaching, and he is also an accomplished pianist. It is safe to suggest that Stewart's most important contribution to the art of the voice is his technique for ridding singers [and actors] of the dreaded nodules that can develop on sensitive vocal cords. He calls himself "a specialist on removing nodules from vocal cords without a knife." After the death of Metropolitan opera baritone and coach Robert Weede, Stewart became voice coach for the American Conservatory Theater under William Ball.

"One instance of Sid Grauman's unfailing kindness is exemplified by an unusual incident that took place during the run of *Noah's Ark*, " Stewart recalls.

A small girl in the Prologue had to stand between two elephants onstage, which so terrified her that she was often in tears onstage and was finally discharged. She came sobbing to me, saying that she was the sole support of her sister and her ailing mother, and now she was out of work. I prevailed upon my mother to speak to Mr. Grauman about her. I remember Mr. Grauman's secretary opening his office door wearing a very long, very theatrical moustache, obviously not his own. My mother entered the office, and as she closed the door her opening words were, "Now look here, Sid—" When my mother emerged minutes later the little girl had her job back and went on in show business to become the famous and talented Julie Hayden who starred in Tennessee Williams' *The Glass Menagerie* on Broadway with the immortal Laurette Taylor, already dying of cancer.

Stewart says that Grauman would sometimes do odd things on a whim. One night Sid routed Stewart and his mother out of bed to hurry down to the theater and into costume without makeup so that he could alter a sequence in the *King of Kings* Prologue. It was 2:30 in the morning. When Mrs. Brady pointed out to Sid that this was quite a trying experience for a young boy, Grauman said he was very sorry. It wouldn't happen again; he had gotten carried away. And it never did happen again.

Sid, Stewart points out, was the rarest of perfectionists. He would often spend a whole day on lighting a single momentary mood in a scene, never resting until he got what he wanted.

"There has never been lighting, even with to-day's technical advances, that could match the beauty and subtlety of Grauman's work," avers Stewart. "This plus his sharp attention to set coloration and costuming. For instance his marvelous use of blues and greens against whites, designed for *King of Kings* by Adrian, were something none of us had ever seen before, but only a part of what made his Prologues unrivalled by productions anywhere. There was a special atmosphere he could evoke in a scene that made it as compelling as a classical painting. When I attend many performances today I often think, but oh, what about the lighting? None of it can equal what Grauman caught. He was an amazing man. I might say a genius."

During the run of the Prologue for *King of Kings*, Stewart was unhappy with the costume he wore as the singing shepherd lad. It was a skin. "I thought it looked like a dress," says Stewart,

so one day I decided to take it off. My mother wasn't in the dressing room at the time, and all I had on was this little pair of black ragged shorts I wore underneath the skin. I decided to go on just like that. Well, when I got down to go onstage, the wardrobe man who always inspected everything before you went on told me I couldn't appear like that. I said why not, and he said it wasn't right. I made a big fuss. So, what did I do? Well, just as soon as the lights went out—my cue to run onstage—the wardrobe man made a grab for me but I slipped away and took my position. As I came down the temple steps to sing, I heard someone in the audience laughing. I went ahead and sang anyway, and afterwards I was given word that Mr. Grauman wanted to see me. I was ready. I entered his office protesting that I hated the costume, etc., etc. . . . But Mr. Grauman stopped my tirade saying, "Now listen, Stewart, if you can come out on stage without anything and get by with it, you do it." And from that time on I never went back to the skin costume again.

One day Stewart inadvertently missed a performance. "My watch was wrong and I didn't have an understudy. What they did to cover my absence I can't recall, but I thought Mr. Grauman would dock me, but he didn't. I was out in the forecourt looking at the footprints when an usherette asked me if I weren't singing that day. And when I said yes, of course, she said it was already past the time of my entrance. Mr. Grauman didn't even comment to me, probably because he knew I was deeply embarrassed by the experience and wouldn't let it happen again. I didn't, of course."

For the past ten years, Stewart Brady has augmented a busy schedule of private coaching to devote a major portion of his energies to the needs of the American Conservatory Theater. He is a dynamic teacher and pianist, and a warm, sensitive human being. He feels that his life was infinitely enriched by his association with Sid Grauman and the Chinese Theater Prologues experience. An early milestone, his two appearances in the Pro-

logues for *King of Kings* and *Noah's Ark* remain vividly with him as cherished memories.

"They inspired me," says Stewart. "Without a doubt Sid Grauman was a powerful influence in my life. He made a lasting contribution to American theatrical history. He brought style and class to the Prologues that introduced most of Hollywood's greatest early triumphs and unquestionably helped to bring the cinema of age. He will always have an important and very special niche in the Hollywood Hall of Fame."

A 1928 portrait of Sid Grauman by the Witzel Studios.

Index

Fitzmaurice, George, 86
Five Mavellos, the, 120
Fleming, Rhonda, 23
Fortune, Louise, 34
Fox, Virgil (organist), 77
Fox, William, 33, 93, 94
Francis, Alec, 75
Franklin, H. B., 117
Frederick, Pauline, 45
French, Edna, 76

Gable, Clark, 24, 120, 121
Gambarelli, Maria, 125
Garbo, Greta, 120, 123, 125, 132
Garland, Judy, 120
Garson, Greer, 23
Gaynor, Janet, 115
Geary, Maine, 83
Gilbert, Billy, 126
Gilbert, John, 24, 96, 97, 98
Gibbons, Cedric, 135
Gilmore, Margalo, 119
Gish, Dorothy, 92
Gish, Lillian, 92, 95
Givot, George, 114
Glazer, Benjamin, 135
Goldwyn, Samuel, 9, 44, 61
Gomez and Winona, 120
Grable, Betty, 23
Grant, Cary, 123
Grauman, David J. (Sid's father), 17, 18, 26, 27, 28, 29, 33, 34, 35, 40, 42, 59, 63, 128, 137
Grauman, Rosa (Sid's mother), 17, 26, 27, 28, 42, 92, 128, 137
Grav, Gilda. 77
Great Creatore (the conductor), 76
Gregor, Nora, 120
Griffith, David Wark, 18, 24, 42, 53, 54, 92, 104, 115
Gross, Milt, 115
Gumm Sisters, the, 120
Gunter, Frank, 130
Guterson, Mischa (conductor), 51, 54, 58

Haggin, Ben Ali, 76
Hale, Alan, 83, 88
Hall, Ben, 74
Hall, James, 117
Hall, Jon, 23
Hanneford, Poodles, 112
Hanson, Lars, 92
Harlow, Jean, 117, 121, 123
Harrison, Ruth, 123
Hart, Moss, 119
Hart, William S., 42, 45, 46, 73, 129
Hatton, Raymond, 76, 86
Haver, Phyllis, 55, 101
Havoc, June, 45, 57
Hayakawa, Sessue, 42, 45
Hayden, Julie, 138
Hays, Will, 18
Helgesen, Terry (theater historian), 108, 109, 110, 116, 132, 133
Heller, Herman S. (conductor), 76, 77
Heming, Violet, 62
Henie, Sonja, 23
Hepburn, Katharine, 123
Hersholt, Jean, 22, 123, 127
Hiers, Walter, 76
Hill, Doris, 77
Hines, Harry, 61
Hitler, Adolf, 122
Holmes, Burton, 57
Holmes, Phillips, 123
Holmes, Stuart, 42

Holt, Jack, 69, 75, 135
Hopper, Hedda, 101
Horton, Edward Everett, 115
Hough, Emerson, 87
Hovick (Havoc), June, 44, 45, 57
Hovick, Rose, 57
Howard, Leslie, 119
Howard, Willie and Eugene, 101
Hughes, Howard, 117, 130
Hughes, Rupert, 9
Hugo, Victor, 115
Huling, Ray, 123
Hunter, Bee, 85
Hurok, Sol, 64

Ince, Thomas, 42, 75
Iribe, Paul, 90

Janis, Elsie, 101
Jessel, George, 101
Johnson, Julius K. (organist), 95
Johnston, Julanne, 82
Jolson, Al, 9, 17, 23, 29, 101, 104, 126
Joplin Kiddies/dancers, 120
Joy, Leatrice, 76, 90

Kahanamoku, Duke, 102
Kauffman, George, 119
Kaufman, Albert, 49, 77
Kay, Arthur (conductor), 51, 56, 112
Keaton, Buster, 75
Kennedy, Merna, 113
Kennedy, Raymond (architect), 109, 110
Kenyon, Doris, 54
Kerrigan, J. Warren, 42, 75, 88
King, Charles, 116
King, Henry, 135
Klossner, Jean, 22
Kobin, Leopold (conductor), 76
Kohler, Fred, 94
Kopp, Rudolph G. (conductor), 42, 44, 51, 76
Koshetz Ukranian Singers, 102
Kosloff, Theodore, 76, 86
Kyne, Peter B., 86

La Rocque, Rod, 89
Lamour, Dorothy, 23
Lanterman, Frank (organist), 116
Lasky, Jesse, 9, 24, 42, 43, 44, 72, 75, 80, 82, 87, 102, 127
Laughlin, Homer, 34, 35, 36, 75
Laurel and Hardy, 117
Laurel, Stan, 32
Lawrence, Florence, 87, 88, 89, 90, 119, 126, 133
Lawrence, Gertrude, 100
Le Berthen, Ted, 51
Leaf, Edward G., 67
Lee and Shaw, 120
Lee, Gypsy Rose, 45, 57
Lee, Jane and Katherine, 76
Lee, Lila, 33, 46, 76
Leisen, James Mitchell, 82
Liebold, Rudolf, 22
Lillie, Beatrice, 100
Linne, H. S., 47
Lloyd, Doris, 76
Lloyd, Frank, 135
Lloyd, Harold, 23, 61, 75, 77, 135
Lockhart, June, 27
Loder, John, 77
Loew, Marcus, 17
London, Jack, 17
Long, Walter, 86